"Danny Akin has written a po[...] most explosive material on missi[...] sionaries who have shaped the modern movement to take the gospel to the nations. I was greatly moved by this book, and you will be, too. Read this book, and pray that the next edition tells the stories of thousands who similarly changed the world."

—R. Albert Mohler, Jr., President,
The Southern Baptist Theological Seminary

"God sends reminders to us through a variety of means. For me, His reminders come to place me gently but firmly back on the path of His will. Frankly, I find myself distracted and often focused on peripheral matters. I need His reminders of what really matters. It is rare that a book has such a profound impact upon my life that I leave its reading with a certainty that I have known the nudge of God. But when I finished *Ten Who Changed the World*, I found myself near the point of tears. Above all, I came away from my reading pleading with Him to take my wretched life and shape it that I might be used, even if only slightly, like these heroes of the faith. Read this book with a warning: You will be moved; and your life may be inalterably changed."

—Thom S. Rainer, President and CEO,
LifeWay Christian Resources

"*Ten Who Changed the World* is not just a book about missionaries, but a book about shepherding a mission-driven heart. Danny Akin's zeal for missions shines through as he reintroduces heroes of the faith in history for the purpose of raising up new ones. *Ten Who Changed the World* is not for armchair theologians, but for those who are ready to 'go and do likewise.'"

—Ed Stetzer, President of LifeWay Research

"Inspiring, encouraging, and challenging all at the same time. In *Ten Who Changed the World* you will be introduced to lives lived for Christ and others. These lives model lives lived with an eternity perspective. Read and you will purchase copies for all you invest in."

—Johnny Hunt, Pastor, First Baptist Church,
Woodstock, Georgia

"Reading any page in this book can kindle a fire in your bones. In this volume, Danny Akin introduces us to ten people who refused to accept a world where the kingship of Jesus isn't announced and embraced all over the globe. Be warned; while reading this book you will probably want to pack it with you and go tell the unreached nations about the One who upends the world and saves it."

—Russell D. Moore, Dean,
The Southern Baptist Theological Seminary

"My life has been enriched by two categories of gospel-centered resources: expositional teaching and missionary biographies. In *Ten Who Changed the World* readers get a remarkable convergence of the two! The pages of this book are filled with eternal truths that are lived out in the power of the Holy Spirit for the glory of God among the nations. The common theme of each chapter is that our extraordinary God delights to use ordinary people in spreading the good news of the gospel through all sorts of circumstances. Dr. Daniel Akin has gifted the church with a resource that will both reinforce her dependency upon Christ and His Word, while inspiring her to follow in the footsteps of some famous, and others not so famous, missionaries who lived to see King Jesus worshipped among the nations."

—Dr. George G. Robinson, Richard and Gina Headrick
Chair of World Missions, Assistant Professor of Missions and
Evangelism, Southeastern Baptist Theological Seminary

"This is a readable and enjoyable biographical introduction to some great Christian leaders. We really enjoyed this book and will be giving away numerous copies."
—Mark Driscoll, Pastor, Mars Hill Church, Seattle, Washington, and his teenage daughter Ashley Driscoll

"From my earliest days in ministry, I developed the habit of reading the biographies of great Christians. Their lives have been used by God to inspire, convict, and challenge me. This collection of biographical messages on valiant soldiers of Christ will do this tenfold. Read this, and get every believer you know to read it as well!"
—Dr. Alvin L. Reid, Professor of Evangelism and Student Ministry/Bailey Smith Chair of Evangelism, Southeastern Baptist Theological Seminary

"In a terrific blending of exciting history and inspiring exposition, Dr. Akin has provided the church with a picture of ten people who really did change the world for the better along with the biblical passage best exemplifying why they did. This is one heartwarming read."
—James Merritt, Lead Pastor, Cross Pointe Church Duluth, Georgia

"As a lover of rich and readable biography, I thank God for this expanded explosion of inspiration."
—John Piper, Pastor for Preaching and Vision, Bethlehem Baptist Church, Minneapolis, Minnesota

"My friend Danny Akin is a skilled Bible teacher dedicated to the cause of international missions. In this book he skillfully weaves together biblical exposition with stories of missionaries who sacrificed their lives to spread the good news of the gospel around the world. These ten compelling biographies will stir your soul ten times over, inspiring you to pray, give, and if called, go for the sake of the gospel."
—C. J. Mahaney, Sovereign Grace Ministries

"All of us need heroes, and this is a book about heroes. These men and women are heroes because they served the Lord with all their might. They are heroes because they would never want to be known as heroes—they would want all the praise directed to Christ. Wrapped in teachings from the Word of God, these stories will challenge you, move you, and inspire you. Read them, and be prepared to go to the nations."

—Chuck Lawless, Ph.D., vice president for
Global Theological Advance, International
Mission Board and Distinguished Professor of
Evangelism and Church Growth,
The Southern Baptist Theological Seminary

"Warning . . . these stories will fly off the pages and penetrate your heart. *Ten Who Changed the World* is definitely a must-read and undoubtedly one that every pastor will want to recommend to his congregation. If we dare grasp the truths in this book, we will indeed change the world. I continue to thank God for the mind and heart of Danny Akin."

—Mike Buster, executive pastor,
Prestonwood Baptist Church, Plano, Texas

"Christian biography is a gift from God to the church, recounting the faithfulness and foibles of ordinary men and women who, by God's grace, became those of whom the world is not worthy. Think of this book as a spread of ten appetizers, whetting your appetite for more. Dr. Akin skillfully weaves the life and lessons from ten missionaries with a key text from Scripture. I expect that the Lord will use this warm and winsome book to encourage and inspire many readers to reach the nations for the glory of God."

—Justin Taylor, blogger, Between Two Worlds

DANIEL L. AKIN

foreword by DAVID PLATT

NEW YORK TIMES BEST-SELLING AUTHOR

10
Who Changed the World

B&H
PUBLISHING GROUP

NASHVILLE, TENNESSEE

978-1-4336-7307-8

Published by B&H Publishing Group
Nashville, Tennessee

Dewey Decimal Classification: 266.092
Subject Heading: MISSIONARIES \ MISSIONS \
MISSIONS IN THE BIBLE

1 2 3 4 5 6 7 8 • 15 14 13 12

Dedication

This book is dedicated to Southeastern Baptist Theological Seminary International Church Planting students, who change the world every day.

Contents

Acknowledgments

Ten Who Changed the World grew out of a series of chapel messages that I preached at Southeastern Baptist Theological Seminary in Wake Forest, North Carolina. I was initially inspired to pursue such a series by the wonderful biographical studies done by John Piper at his Desiring God Pastors Conference. Expounding a biblical text, I used the lives, writings and experiences of great missionaries to serve as illustrations throughout the messages. The response and feedback was far more than I ever imagined, and I am grateful for God's undeserved blessing.

I am especially indebted in this project to Tanner Turley, Michael Guyer, Kim Humphrey, and Debbie Shugart for their service in research and typing of the manuscripts. They are all the best!

In addition, I have received great encouragement from missionaries and missionary professors like Jerry Rankin, Tom Elliff, Gordon Fort, Chuck Lawless, Zane Pratt, Bruce Ashford, George Robinson, Scott Hildreth, Greg Mathias, Joseph Solc, and Al James. I am also thankful for Richard and Gina Headrick who took Charlotte and me to six countries in fourteen days. My burden for the nations was never the same after that.

I am also thankful for my four sons and their wives, each of whom has a great love and passion for the nations. They all are consumed with a desire to make King Jesus famous among the nations. I am so very proud of each and every one.

Also, a big thank-you goes to B&H and in particular my dear friends Thom Rainer, Brad Waggoner, and Jedidiah Coppenger. Your support and encouragement in all of this was always there. You guys are a tremendous gift to the body of Christ.

Finally, I want to say thank you to my wife Charlotte who is the love of my life. Not only has she loved, cared for, and supported me for more than three decades, she has also gone with me again and again to the ends of the earth on mission assignments. I am a better servant of King Jesus because of the special lady God put in my life.

Foreword

by David Platt

Apart from the Bible, the most profitable books I have read in my spiritual journey are personal biographies, particularly the stories of saints who have gone before us.

I remember how my perspective on the Christian life fundamentally changed when I first read about the life of Jim Elliot. He and his four missionary comrades were murdered on an Ecuadorian beachhead by the men they sought to reach with the gospel. The words from Elliot's journal still resound in my head: "Consider the call from the Throne above, 'Go ye,' and from round about, 'Come over and help us,' and even the call from the damned souls below, 'Send Lazarus to my brothers, that they come not to this place.' Impelled, then, by these voices, I dare not stay home while Quichuas perish."

I remember my introduction to Adoniram Judson, who spent thirty-eight years of his life in Buddhist Burma. He suffered through cholera, malaria, dysentery, and unknown other miseries that would claim the lives of his first wife, second wife, and seven of his thirteen children, as well as numerous colleagues. Yet he persevered, and today Burma has hundreds of thousands of believers spread across that country.

I remember getting my first glimpse of William Carey's heart in his *Enquiry into the Obligations of Christians to Use Means for the Conversion of the Heathen*. Carey passionately maintained that it was the solemn obligation of the church to take the gospel to those who have never heard. He later preached his well-known deathless sermon consisting of two main points: expect great things from God and attempt great things for God. Soon thereafter, the Baptist Missionary Society was formed, and in the words of one historian, "The world has never been quite the same since."

This is truly the testimony of these saints and countless others like them: the world is different because of them. More appropriately, the world is different because of God's work in them. Throughout history God has used ordinary people to accomplish his extraordinary purposes. He has bestowed great grace on certain individuals for the sake of his glory among entire peoples.

The stories of these saints are not intended simply to inform us about how God has worked in the past. They are given by God to inspire us concerning how he is working in the present. For the same Holy Spirit that filled Jim Elliot, Adoniram Judson, William Carey, David Brainerd, George Leile, Lottie Moon, James Fraser, Eric Liddell, John and Betty Stam, and William Wallace is the same Holy Spirit who dwells in every follower of Christ. And He desires to use your life and mine in multiplied ways to make His majestic glory known to the ends of the earth.

For this reason we are indebted to my dear friend, Danny Akin. In this book he has brought the lives of ten such saints to our attention. He has uniquely told their stories through the lens of scriptural truth that saturated each of their lives.

The result is a book that is historical and biblical, concise and challenging, personal and penetrating. My prayer is that the truth of God will come alive in your heart through the stories of these saints, to the end that you will be compelled to spend your life, without condition and regardless of cost, making the glory of our great God known throughout the world.

—David Platt
Author of *Radical: Taking Back
Your Faith from the American Dream*

Foreword

by Bruce Ashford

Missions matters because God is a missionary God. Therefore, his people must be a missionary people. From Genesis to Revelation, we see God's central promise that he would send Messiah, and that Messiah will win the nations unto himself. Through Messiah God's glory will cover the earth. Through Messiah the lost will be saved.

And yet almost two billion people have little or no access to Messiah. Many corners of the globe have no churches, no Bibles, and no Christians to bear testimony. Many of these two billion people could leave their homes and search—for days and weeks and months—and never find a Christian, a Bible, or a church. It is our responsibility to remedy this. Our Lord commands us in Matthew 28:18–20 to make disciples of *all* nations.

The magnitude of this task is great, but it is matched and exceeded by the magnitude of our biblical convictions: that God is a missionary God; that all people without Christ are lost; that a central theme in the Scriptures is God's desire to win the nations unto himself; that since the coming of his Son, God has chosen that all saving faith be consciously focused on Christ; that the church's task in each generation is to proclaim the gospel to her generation; and that this progress of the gospel to the ends of the earth may be hindered temporarily, but there can be no doubt about its final triumph.

In Revelation 5 our Lord gives John a breathtaking vision. In this vision all of heaven bursts forth into praise. Among those worshipping, John sees men and women from every tribe, tongue, people, and nation. This is the vision that drives us—that our Lord will be worshipped from all corners of the globe. He alone is worthy of such worship. Our lives should be lived in such a way as to contribute to this triumphant march of God, as he draws unto himself worshippers from every tribe, tongue, people, and nation.

This is the driving passion behind this series of missions messages preached by Danny Akin and collected in this book. In each message he couples a passage of Scripture with a missionary biography. As he preaches through Matthew 28:16–20; Romans 8:28–39; Philippians 1:21; Romans 12:1; Psalm 96; Revelation 5:8–10; 2 Timothy 1:8–12; Galatians 6:11–18; Psalm 67; and Hebrews 12:1–3, he expounds and illustrates those same passages with riveting lessons and stories from the lives of William Carey, Adoniram Judson, William Wallace, Lottie Moon, Jim Elliot, James Fraser, David Brainerd, George Leile, John and Betty Stam, and Eric Liddell.

Be forewarned, however. This book is for those who like their coffee strong. Those who read these messages will find themselves informed, rebuked, challenged, and motivated. They may even find themselves able to say, as Jim Elliot does in the pages of this book, that "he is no fool who gives what he cannot keep to gain that which he cannot lose."

—Bruce Riley Ashford
Dean of the College at Southeastern
Associate Professor of Theology and Culture
Southeastern Baptist Theological Seminary
Wake Forest, North Carolina

CHAPTER 1

The Great Commission and William Carey: A Passionate Global Vision

Matthew 28:16–20

 William Carey may have been the greatest missionary since the time of the apostles. He rightly deserves the honor of being known as "the father of the modern missions movement." Carey was born in 1761, and he left England in 1793 as a missionary to India. He would never return home again, instead dying in 1834 among the people he had given his life to save.

William Carey was poor, with only a grammar school education, and yet he would translate the Bible into dozens of languages and dialects. He established schools and mission stations all over India. Timothy George (dean of Beeson Divinity School) described Carey as a "lone, little man. His resume would have read: Education—minimal. Degrees—

none. Savings—depleted. Political influence—nil. References—a band of country preachers half a world away. What were Carey's resources? Weapon—love. Desire—to bring the light of God into the darkness. Strategy—to proclaim by life, lips, and letters the unsearchable riches of Christ."[1]

William Carey understood Matthew 28:16–20. It was his farewell text to his church at Harvey Lane before departing to India. Though he had been rebuked earlier by the respected minister John Ryland Sr., Carey was undeterred. Ryland had told him, with his now infamous words, "Young man, sit down. When God pleases to convert the heathen, He will do without your aid or mine."[2] Despite this he would powerfully proclaim, "Expect great things. Attempt great things." (Later tradition would add "from God" and "for God," though this is undoubtedly what he meant.)[3]

He would publish his famous *An Enquiry into the Obligations of Christians to Use Means for the Conversion of the Heathens.*[4] Here he would pen searing words for the church of his day as well as our own. Commenting on the Great Commission text, found in Matthew 28:16–20, Carey wrote:

> This commission was as extensive as possible, and laid them under obligation to disperse themselves into every country to the habitable globe, and preach to all the inhabitants, without exception, or limitation. They accordingly went forth in obedience to the command, and the power of God evidently wrought with them. Many attempts of the same kind have been made since their day, and which have been attended with various success; but the work has not been taken up, or prosecuted of late years (except by a few individuals) with that zeal and perseverance with which the primitive Christians went about it. It seems as if

many thought the commission was sufficiently put in execution by what the apostles and others have done; that we have enough to do to attend to the salvation of our own countrymen; and that, if God intends the salvation of the heathen, he will some way or other bring them to the gospel, or the gospel to them. It is thus that multitudes sit at ease, and give themselves no concern about the far greater part of their fellow sinners, who to this day, are lost in ignorance and idolatry.[5]

Carey would later add, "I question whether all are justified in staying here, while so many are perishing without means of grace in other lands."[6]

The words found in Matthew 28 constitute the last words of Jesus in this Gospel. They are intended to be lasting words and the final marching orders for Christ's followers until he returns. I once heard Adrian Rogers in a sermon say that in this passage we find "the heartbeat of the Son of God." Here we are told that "we are all to bring all men by all means to Jesus by any cost."

Acknowledge He Has All Power (Matt. 28:16–18)

The eleven disciples minus Judas go north to Galilee "to the mountain where Jesus had told them to go" (v. 16 NIV). The scene is reminiscent of the setting of the Sermon on the Mount (Matt. 5:1). It is interesting to note that the climatic temptation (Matt 4:8–11), the Sermon on the Mount (Matt. 5–7), the transfiguration (Matt. 17:1), the Olivet Discourse prophecy (Matt. 24–25), and now the Great Commission of the Great King all took place on a mountain.

Suddenly they see the resurrected, risen Lord. What transpires is instructive for our careful consideration and response.

Worship Him (Matt. 28:17)

Seeing him the people worship. Amazingly though, some still doubt. Did they have doubts as to whether or not they should worship this man? Perhaps. Were their doubts in confusion about the whole thing? Perhaps. Did the people doubt because they did not know how to respond given their past failures and track record? Almost certainly.

Even in the midst of their doubts, worship is the wise and right thing to do. Even when I may not understand all he is doing in my life, *worship.* If I am confused, unsure and hesitating, *worship.* When I am sorrowful, heartbroken, and crushed, *worship.* Am I discouraged, depressed, and in utter despair? *Worship.* Even when I am at death's door? *Worship!*

On his deathbed, Carey breathed to the Scottish missionary Alexander Duff, "When I am gone, say nothing about Dr. Carey. Speak about Dr. Carey's Savior."[7] Jesus is the Savior so worship him.

Hear Him (Matt. 28:18)

Jesus said, "All authority is mine, in heaven and on earth." Satan offered Jesus an earthly kingdom, but His Father planned so much more (Matt. 4:8–11). The words echo the great Son of Man text where the Bible declares of this heavenly, divine Man, "Then to Him was given dominion and glory and a kingdom, that all peoples, nations, and languages should serve Him. His dominion is an everlasting dominion, which shall not pass away, and His kingdom the one which shall not be destroyed" (Dan. 7:14 NKJV). John Piper gets to the heart of these words and says:

> Here we see the *peak of power.* Notice verse 18. Jesus says, "All authority in heaven and on earth has been given to me." If you gathered all the authority of all the

governments and armies of the world and put them on the scales with the authority of the risen Christ, they would go up in the balance like air. *All authority* on earth has been given to the risen Christ. *All* of it! The risen Christ has the right to tell every man, woman, and child on this planet today what they should do and think and feel. He has absolute and total authority over your life and over cities and states and nations. The risen Christ is great—greater than you have ever imagined.

Here is our witness to the world: The risen Christ is your king and has absolute, unlimited authority over your life. If you do not bow and worship him and trust him and obey him, you commit high treason against Christ the King, who is God over all. The resurrection is God's open declaration that he lays claim on every person and tribe and tongue and nation . . . "All authority on earth is mine." Your sex life is his to rule; your business is his to rule; your career is his to rule; your home is his; your children are his; your vacation is his; your body is his. He is *God*! So if you resist his claim, feel no admiration for his infinite power and authority, and turn finally to seek satisfaction from thrills that allow you to be your own master, then you will be executed for treason in the last day. And it will appear so reasonable and so right that you should be executed for your disloyalty to your Maker and Redeemer that there will be no appeals and no objections. Your life of indifference to the risen Christ and of halfhearted attention now and then to a few of his commandments will appear on that day as supremely blameworthy and infinitely foolish, and you will . . . weep that you did not change."[8]

Obey His Authoritative Plan (*Matt. 28:19–20*)

Commenting on Matthew 28:19, John Calvin wrote, "Now the wall is pulled down and the Lord orders the ministers of the gospel to go far out to scatter the teaching of salvation throughout all the regions of the earth."[9] Tragically many in Carey's day, as well as our own, have imbibed the spirit of the eighteenth-century antimissions hymn: *Go into all the world, the Lord of old did say. But now where He has planted thee, there thou shouldst stay.*[10]

Carey would have no part of this spiritually bankrupt and impotent thinking. Rather, having his heart gripped by the words of our Savior, he said: "I care not where or how I lived, or what hardships I went through, so that I could but gain souls for Christ. While I was asleep I dreamed of these things, and when I awoke the first thing I thought of was this great work. All my desire was for the conversion of the heathen, and all my hope was in God."[11]

The imperative or command of verse 19 is "make disciples." The "therefore" links the command to the "all authority" declaration of verse 18. Further, wed to an imperative, the three participles—going, baptizing, and teaching—receive the force and thrust of imperatives. Thus Jesus charges us, commands us to make disciples by going, make disciples by baptizing, and make disciples by teaching.

Make Disciples by Going (Matt. 28:19)

There is no need to pray and ask God if we should go and take the gospel to the nations. We have been told to go. Again, John Piper says:

So there you have the word of God from the mouth of Jesus. The lofty claim: "All authority is given to me." The loving comfort: "I am with you always, even to the end of the age." The last command: "Go make disciples among all the peoples of the world." What is clear from this final word of Jesus is that he is trying to move us to act. He not only says, "Go make disciples." He also gives us a warrant for doing it so that we can know it is a legitimate and right thing to do: All authority in heaven and on earth is his. He gives us tremendous encouragement and comfort and strength to go, with the promise that he would go with us and never leave us. Jesus ended his earthly life with these words because he wanted us to respond. He was motivating us to act.[12]

Do you need a reason to go? No! You need a reason to stay! More than 1.6 billion people have yet to hear the name of Jesus.

R. T. France captures the theological thrust of Jesus' command to go when he says, "Jesus' vision of the future heavenly enthronement of the Son of Man in Matthew 24:30 led naturally into a mission to gather his chosen people from all over the earth (24:31). . . . But the agents of this ingathering are not now to be angels . . . but those who are already Jesus' disciples."[13]

Go and make more followers, more disciples of Jesus. Where? All the nations.

In his journal entry on March 29, 1794, Carey wrote, "O what is there in all this world worth living for but the presence and service of God—I feel a burning desire that all the world may know this God and serve Him."[14]

Go and make disciples.

Make Disciples by Baptizing (Matt. 28:19)

Here is the badge of being a disciple. Here is where biblical profession of faith takes place. Here is my unashamed identification with Jesus as my Lord by public declaration.

Baptism—immersion, plain and clear.

Name—singular.

Father, Son, and Holy Spirit—Father, Savior, and Comforter, the Triune God.

What joy to initiate new believers into the church of the Lord Jesus as they identify themselves with Christ in death, burial, and resurrection. And that they would be found in every nation and from all the peoples of the earth! What a gospel! What a mission! What an assignment!

Closing his *Enquiry* with a word of missionary encouragement, Carey wrote: "What a heaven will it be to see the many myriads of poor heathens . . . who by their labors have been brought to the knowledge of God. Surely a 'crown of rejoicing' (1 Thess. 2:19) like this is worth aspiring to. Surely it is worth while to lay ourselves out with all our might in promoting the cause and kingdom of Christ."[15]

Make Disciples by Teaching (Matt. 28:20)

We do not make converts. We are called to make disciples, "little Christs," who observe all his teachings. James Boice well says, "Robust disciples are not made by watered-down teaching."[16] A "hit and run" approach to missions and ministry will fail to accomplish this. Short-term endeavors, though commendable and valuable, are no substitute for those who give years, even the rest of their lives, to teach others who can teach others who can teach others.

Baptism is preschool enrollment into a school of learning that one never graduates from! But someone must go and teach them.

Trust His Amazing Promise (Matt. 28:20)

William Carey was a great man, but he was a man. Life brought him many tragedies. Francis Wayland said of him, "Like most of the master minds of all ages, Carey was educated in the school of adversity."[17] There were times when his soul was plunged to the depths of depression. He would bury two wives, with his first, Dorothy, sorrowfully, going insane. He would bury three children, and certain others disappointed him. He lost most of his hair due to illness in his early twenties, served in India for forty-one years never taking a furlough, fought back dysentery and malaria, and did not baptize his first Indian convert, Krisha Pal, until his seventh year on the field! What kept him going? What promise of God did he claim again and again in the face of discouragement and defeat? He had asked his friend John Williams in 1801, "Pray for us that we may be faithful to the end."[18] He was! How? This promise: "And lo, I am with you always, even to the end of the age" (Matt. 28:20 NKJV).

Two aspects to this amazing promise sustained Carey, and they will sustain us as well wherever the Lord might send us.

He will be with you constantly ("always"). He will be with you continually ("to the end of the age"). Knowing God was with him constantly and continually saw Carey through those valleys of the shadow of death, dungeons of despair, and feelings of total inadequacy. In a letter to his father he wrote concerning his call:

> I see more and more of my own insufficiency for the great work I am called to. The truths of God are amazingly profound, the souls of men infinitely precious, my own ignorance very great and all that I do is for God who knows my motives and my ends, my diligence or negligence. When I (in short) compare myself with my work, I sink into a point, a mere despicable nothing.[19]

In his journal entry dated August 27–31, 1794, Carey wrote:[20]

August 27

Nothing new, my Soul is in general barren and unfruitful; yet I find a pleasure in drawing near to God; and a peculiar sweetness in His Holy Word. I find it more & more to be a very precious treasure.

August 28–30

Nothing of any importance except to my shame, a prevalence of carnality, negligence, and spiritual deadness; no heart for private duties, indeed everything seems to be going to decay in my soul, and I almost despair of being any use to the heathen at all.

August 31

Was somewhat engaged more than of late in the things of God, felt some new devotedness to God, and desired to live entirely to him, and for his glory; O that I could live always as under his eye, and feel a sense of his immediate presence, this is life and all besides this is death to my soul.

G. Campbell Morgan was reading Matthew 28:20 to an eighty-five-year-old saint. Finishing the verse he said: "'That is a great promise.' She looked up and said sharply, with the light of sanctified humor in her eyes; 'That is not a promise at all, that is a fact. Oh, if the church of God could remember that fact!'"[21]

Conclusion

Matthew 28 begins with a resurrection and ends with a commission. These final words of our Lord are weighty, heavy, and not easily digested. They do not need an adrenalin response. They need a cardiac response, a heart response. They need a response that has carefully considered the King who speaks them, and the kind of servant who obeys them. Once more hear the words of William Carey, who heard and heeded His Master's call.

> A Christian minister is a person who is "not his own" (1 Cor. 6:19); he is the servant of God, and therefore ought to be wholly devoted to him. By entering on that sacred office he solemnly undertakes to be always engaged as much as possible in the Lord's work, and not to choose his own pleasure or employment, or pursue the ministry as something that is to subserve his own ends or interest, or as a kind of sideline. He engages to go where God pleases, and to do or endure what he sees fit to command or call him to in the exercise of his function. He virtually bids farewell to friends, pleasures, and comforts, and stands in readiness to endure the greatest sufferings in the work of the Lord, his Master. It is inconsistent for ministers to please themselves with thoughts of numerous congregations, cordial friends, a civilized country, legal protection, affluence, splendor, or even an income that is sufficient. The slights and hatred of men, and even pretended friends, gloomy prisons, and tortures, the society of barbarians of uncouth speech, miserable accommodations in wretched wildernesses, hunger and thirst, nakedness, weariness, and diligence, hard work, and but little worldly encouragement, should

rather be the objects of their expectation. . . . I question whether all are justified in staying here, while so many are perishing without means of grace in other lands. . . . On the contrary the commission is a sufficient call to them to venture all, and, like the primitive Christians, go everywhere preaching the gospel.[22]

On his seventieth birthday, three years before his death, Carey would give his own humble evaluation of his life and ministry. Herein we discover something of the man that made him great for God. In a letter to his son Jabez, he wrote:

I am this day seventy years old, a monument of Divine mercy and goodness, though on a review of my life I find much, very much, for which I ought to be humbled in the dust; my direct and positive sins are innumerable, my negligence in the Lord's work has been great, I have not promoted his cause, nor sought his glory and honor as I ought, notwithstanding all this, I am spared till now, and am still retained in his Work, and I trust I am received into the divine favor through him. I wish to be more entirely devoted to his service, more completely sanctified and more habitually exercising all the Christian graces, and bringing forth the fruits of righteousness to the praise and honor of that Savior who gave his life a sacrifice for sin.[23]

After he died on June 9, 1834, these simple words would be inscribed on the stone slab that marked his grave in Serampore, India: "A wretched, poor, and helpless worm, on thy kind arms I fall."[24] Would to God that he would raise up from among us an army of such wretched, poor, and helpless worms. The world needs them. Jesus deserves them. Our churches should provide them.

CHAPTER 2

Marked for Death, Messengers of Life: Adoniram and Ann Judson[1]

Romans 8:28–39

 Adoniram Judson is the father of the American Baptist missionary movement. Eugene Harrison calls him "the apostle of the love of Christ in Burma."[2]

He left American soil as a Congregationalist. Arriving in India, having carefully studied the New Testament, he became a Baptist. He was baptized by an associate of William Carey. He eventually went to Burma where he labored for nearly forty years. He translated the whole Bible into Burmese, spent twenty-one months in a brutal prison, and buried two wives and more than five children. Divine providence indeed marked him for death, while also making him a messenger of life.

Born in 1788 in Massachusetts, he died in 1850 and was buried at sea. No earthly grave marks his departure from this world into the world of his King Jesus. Fred Barlow said it well when he wrote, "By whatever measurement you measure the man Judson—the measurement always is the same—he was a mighty man!"[3]

Romans 8:28–39 is written all over the life of this wonderful Baptist missionary. Indeed, had he not been confident of the truths contained in these verses, he would have never "finished the race" and "kept the faith" (2 Tim. 4:8). Many of us will likewise be sustained only by the same.

Four lessons leap from this text for our blessing and benefit. Each was marvelously lived out by Adoniram and Ann Judson. Each comes in the form of a divine promise.

We Have His Providence (*Rom. 8:28–32*)

Paul affirms that there are no accidents in the life of the child of God, only providence. In 8:28 we are given a: certain promise (we know); comprehensive promise (all things); comforting promise (work together for good); chosen promise (those who love God); clear promise (called according to his purpose). Paul also affirms the signed, sealed, and settled nature of our salvation through what I like to call the "golden chain of redemption."

The chain has five links, located in verses 29–30. First, God foreknew. Second, he predestined. Third, he called. Fourth, he justified. Fifth, he glorified. These are certain realities in the plan and purpose of God. Such a glorious and certain salvation has definite and wonderful consequences: God is for us (v. 31), and he will give us everything we need for his glory and our good (v. 32).

How did this divine providence work itself out in Judson's life? Let me note three ways.

First, his family and education. Mentally, he was a giant. He began reading at the age of three, took navigation lessons at ten, studied theology as a child, and entered Providence College (now Brown University) at seventeen. Despite the fact that his father was a Congregational preacher, and in spite of his mother's "tears and prayers," Judson was not saved until he was twenty years of age.[4] In college he became a confirmed deist, due largely to the influence of a brilliant unbelieving student at Brown who set out to win Judson to his deistic faith. That man was Jacob Eames of Belfast, Maine. Keep that name in mind.

Second, his conversion. No conversion, save the apostle Paul's, is any more providential in its character than that of Adoniram. After graduation he left home to become a wanderlust (a traveler in search of excitement), confirmed and growing in his deistic convictions. One night while traveling, he stopped to stay in a country inn. His room was adjacent to the room of a dying man. The moaning and groaning of that man through the long night permitted Judson no sleep. His thoughts troubled him. All night questions assailed his soul: "Was the dying man prepared to die? Where would he spend eternity? Was he a Christian, calm and strong in the hope of life in Heaven? Or, was he a sinner shuddering in the dark brink of the lower region?"[5] Judson constantly chided himself for even entertaining such thoughts contrary to his philosophy of life beyond the grave and thought how his brilliant college friend would rebuke him if he learned of these childish worries.

But the next morning, when Judson was leaving, he was informed that the man had died. He inquired of the proprietor as to the identity of the dead man. He was shocked by the staggering statement that he heard: He was a brilliant young person from Providence College. Eames was his name.[6]

Jacob Eames was the unbeliever who had destroyed Judson's faith. "Now he was dead—and was lost! Was lost! Was lost! Lost! Lost!"[7] Those words raced through his brain, rang in his ears, roared in his soul—"Was lost! Lost! Lost!" There and then Judson realized he was lost, too! He immediately ended his traveling, returned home, and entered Andover Theological Seminary. Soon he "sought God for the saving of his soul."[8] Shortly thereafter he was saved, and he dedicated his life to the Master's service!

Joining a group at Andover called "the Brethren," an outgrowth of the famous "Haystack Revival," he would answer God's call to be a missionary. This would lead him to turn down golden opportunities both at Brown and an influential church in Plymouth. The latter broke the heart of his mother who on hearing of the offer rejoiced and said, "And you will be so near home."[9]

Judson, however, replied, "I shall never live in Boston. I have further than that to go." Neither the tears of his mother and sister nor the hopes and dreams of his father could deter him from his call to go to the nations for Jesus' sake.

Third, his wife. God led Judson both to the right woman and, I should add, the right father-in-law. Ann (Nancy) Hasseltine would become the first woman missionary from America to go overseas. She would die at the young age of thirty-seven. The two children she bore (she also miscarried at least once) would die in infancy, Roger Williams at eight months and Maria at twenty-seven months.

Ann was saved at sixteen and married Adoniram when she was twenty-three. Brilliant in her own right, she learned Burmese and Siamese, did translation work, and cared for her husband tirelessly during his imprisonment. There is little doubt this dedication cost Ann her life.

Having been smitten by Ann, Adoniram wrote a letter to her father asking for her hand in marriage and also one to Ann where he lays bare his heart for her and the mission with which God had burdened his soul. Both letters are legendary among missionaries.

The letter to Mr. Hasseltine:

I have now to ask whether you can consent to part with your daughter early next spring, to see her no more in this world? Whether you can consent to her departure to a heathen land, and her subjection to the hardships and sufferings of a missionary life? Whether you can consent to her exposure to the dangers of the ocean; to the fatal influence of the southern climate of India; to every kind of want and distress; to degradation, insult, persecution, and perhaps a violent death? Can you consent to all this, for the sake of Him who left His heavenly home and died for her and for you; for the sake of perishing, immortal souls; for the sake of Zion and the glory of God? Can you consent to all this, in hope of soon meeting your daughter in the world of glory, with a crown of righteousness brightened by the acclamations of praise which shall redound to her Savior from heathens saved, through her means, from eternal woe and despair?[10]

The letter to Ann (January 1, 1811):

It is with the utmost sincerity, and with my whole heart, that I wish you, my love, a happy new year. May it be a year in which your walk will be close with God; your frame calm and serene; and the road that leads you to the Lamb marked with purer light. May

it be a year in which you will have more largely the
spirit of Christ, be raised above sublunary things, and
be willing to be disposed of in this world just as God
shall please. As every moment of the year will bring
you nearer the end of your pilgrimage, may it bring
you nearer to God, and find you more prepared to hail
the messenger of death as a deliverer and a friend. And
now, since I have begun to wish, I will go on. May this
be the year in which you will change your name; in
which you will take a final leave of your relatives and
native land; in which you will cross the wide ocean,
and dwell on the other side of the world, among a
heathen people. What a great change will this year
probably effect in our lives! How very different will
be our situation and employment! If our lives are preserved and our attempt prospered, we shall next new
year's day be in India, and perhaps wish each other a
happy new year in the uncouth dialect of Hindostan or
Burmah. We shall no more see our kind friends around
us, or enjoy the conveniences of civilized life, or go to
the house of God with those that keep holy day; but
swarthy countenances will everywhere meet our eye,
the jargon of an unknown tongue will assail our ears,
and we shall witness the assembling of the heathen to
celebrate the worship of idol gods. We shall be weary
of the world, and wish for wings like a dove, that we
may fly away and be at rest. We shall probably experience seasons when we shall be "exceeding sorrowful,
even unto death." We shall see many dreary, discon-
solate hours, and feel a sinking of spirits, anguish of
mind, of which now we can form little conception.
O, we shall wish to lie down and die. And that time
may soon come. One of us may be unable to sustain

the heat of the climate and the change of habits; and the other may say, with literal truth, over the grave—

"By foreign hands thy dying eyes were closed;
By foreign hands thy decent limbs composed;
By foreign hands thy humble grave adorned."

but whether we shall be honored and mourned by strangers, God only knows. At least, either of us will be certain of *one* mourner. In view of such scenes shall we not pray with earnestness "O for an overcoming faith," etc. ?[11]

Thirteen months later they would marry. A few days after that they sailed for Calcutta on their way, by unseen providence, to Rangoon, Burma. Yes, the child of God has the Lord's providence.

We Have His Prayers (*Rom. 8:33–34*)

The child of God has a double divine blessing in the department of prayer. In verses 26–27 we learn that the Spirit of God prays in us. In verses 33–34 we learn that in heaven the Son of God prays for us. In heart and in heaven, deity intercedes for the child of God.

In verse 33 the theme of our justification is brought forward once again (cf. v. 30). Using a courtroom analogy, Paul points out no one can successfully bring a charge or accusation that will stick against a believer because God has declared us just from his bar as judge.

Verse 34 builds on verse 33 and settles the issue decisively once and for all. Who can charge or condemn us at the judgment with the hope that we will be found guilty? Again the answer is no one! Why? Four reasons are given. First, Christ died [for us]. Second, he is raised [for us]. Third, he is exalted at God's right hand [for us]. Fourth, he continually makes intercession for us (cf. Heb. 7:25).

Hallelujah! What a Savior!

Knowing of the intercession of Jesus was crucial to Judson. Sometimes it was all he had to lean on in the midst of sorrow and suffering. How so?

Arriving in India, the East India Company forced the Judsons to leave as they tried to settle at different places. They lived four months on the Isle of France, where they learned of the death of Mrs. Harriett Newell, Ann's best friend, a nineteen-year-old teen who had sailed with them from America to serve as a fellow missionary. Harriett died while giving birth to her baby girl on the cabin floor of a ship with only her husband at her side. The baby also died, and so would her husband soon thereafter. The Judsons finally found a resting place on July 13, 1812, at Rangoon, Burma. Here, by their sweat, labor, and blood, the gospel would be planted among the hostile Burmese peoples.

In Rangoon the first ten years of missionary labors were given mainly to the mastering of the Burmese language. They had no grammar, dictionary, or English-speaking teacher. Three years after their arrival, Adoniram completed a grammar for the Burmese language. On May 20, 1817, he finished the translation of Matthew; he also wrote tracts—concise, clear statements of Bible truth—and gave them out discriminately and prayerfully.

After almost seven years in Burma, on April 4, 1819, Adoniram ventured to preach his first public discourse. Sitting in a traditional Burmese zayat by the roadside, he would call out, "Ho! Everyone that thirsteth for knowledge!"[12] On June 27 he baptized Moung Hau, his first Burmese convert. Soon others who had also been taught would follow. By 1822 he could count eighteen converts after ten years of laboring.

In 1824 war broke out between Burma and the English government of India, and the Judsons were looked upon as English spies. On June 8, 1824, Judson was arrested and put first in what many called "the Death Prison," the horrible prison of Oung-pen-la. The dimensions of "the Death Prison" were forty by thirty feet, five feet high, with no ventilation other than the cracks between the boards.

In this room were confined one hundred persons of both sexes and all nationalities, nearly all naked, and half famished. The prison was never washed or even swept. Putrid remains of animal and vegetable matter, together with nameless abominations, strewed the floor. In this place of torment, Mr. Judson lay with five pairs of fetters on his legs and ankles, weighing about fourteen pounds, the marks of which he carried to his dying day. At nightfall, lest the prisoners should escape, a bamboo pole was placed between their legs and then drawn up by means of pulleys to a height that allowed only their shoulders to rest on the ground while their feet hung from the iron rings of the fetters.

Mosquitoes would often land and eat away the broken flesh of their feet, nearly driving them mad. Adoniram endured twenty-one months of prison life, nearly dying on several occasions. Of the British POWs, all but one would die.

Judson was not the only sufferer. His wife Ann was without support or protection. Yet she brought food to the prison day after day and with bribes passed the officials and gave relief to her husband and some of the other suffering prisoners. She gave birth to a child, and after twenty-one days carried the little girl in her arms to show to her father in prison. The child contracted smallpox; then the mother herself was inflicted with the same disease, followed closely by spotted fever, which brought her close to death. After many petitions she secured permission for her husband to come out of prison, and he, with fetters on and a guard following, carried their crying baby about the streets, begging Burman mothers to nurse the child. Ann could not nurse her own little girl, she was so emaciated and weak.

During this time Adoniram and Ann tried to remain strong, despite the fact that their health deteriorated and death nearly claimed each of them on numerous occasions. Judson once remarked, "It is possible my life will be spared; if so, with what [zeal] shall I pursue my work! If not—His will be done. The door will be open for others who will do the work better."[13]

Later, toward the end of his imprisonment, his faith would be severely tested. Courtney Anderson summarizes the situation: "His daughter was starving before his eyes; [Ann] was nearly dead, his translation was lost; he himself was marked for death."[14]

I am convinced it was the prayers of the Savior that sustained him during those days.

We Have His Power (Rom. 8:35–37)

Life, by its nature, is filled with sorrow and suffering, hardships and disappointments. Yet, no thing in this life can conquer the child of God. Why? We have his prayers (v. 34) and his love (vv. 37 and 39) which gives us the victory.

In verse 35 Paul notes the realities that will come against but cannot conquer the child of God. In verse 36 he passionately notes the precious lives given for the sake of King Jesus. This destiny was foretold in Psalm 44:22.

Yet in all of this and more, we are "more than conquerors," "super conquerors" through him who loves us. Do you see it? His great power is wedded to and made active by His great love, a power that can keep us going *against all odds!*

Adoniram Judson desperately needed to know this. Eventually he was released from prison. He quickly made his way to Ann and little Maria. Read what he met in the words of Eugene Harrison:

> One of the most pathetic pages in the history of Christian missions is that which describes the scene when Judson was finally released and returned to the mission house seeking Ann, who again had failed to visit him for some weeks. As he ambles down the street as fast as his maimed ankles would permit, the tormenting question kept repeating itself, "Is Ann still alive?" Upon reaching the house, the first object to attract his attention was a fat, half-naked Burman woman squatting in the ashes beside a pan of coals and holding on her knees an emaciated baby, so begrimed with dirt that it did not occur to him that it could be his own. Across the foot of the bed, as though she had fallen there, lay a human object that, at the first glance, was no more recognizable than his child. The face was of a ghastly paleness and the body shrunken to the last degree of emaciation. The glossy black curls had all been shorn from the finely-shaped head. There lay the faithful and devoted wife who had followed him so unwearily from prison to prison, ever alleviating his distresses and consoling him in his trials. Presently Ann felt warm tears falling upon her face and, rousing from her daze, saw Adoniram at her side.[15]

She suffered from spotted fever and cerebral meningitis. Amazingly she survived but only briefly. In less than a year, while away out of necessity, he received what is known as "the blacked sealed letter."[16] Told by its deliverer that he was sorry to inform Adoniram of the death of his little Maria, he opened the letter only to read: "My Dear Sir: To one who has suffered so much and with such exemplary fortitude, there needs but little preface to tell a tale of distress. It was cruel indeed to torture you with doubt and suspense. To sum up the unhappy tidings in a few words—Mrs. Judson is no more."[17]

Ann had died a month earlier while he was away. His beautiful and faithful helper had gone to be with her King. Six months later, on April 24, 1827, little Maria slipped into eternity and into the arms of Jesus, united so quickly with her mother.

Death seemed to be all about Adoniram. For a period of months he was plunged into despair and depression. He would flee to the jungle and live the life of a hermit, for some time questioning himself, his calling, even his faith. He demanded all his letters to America be destroyed.[18] He renounced the D.D. degree bestowed upon him by Brown.

He gave all his private wealth, a sizable sum, to the Baptist Mission Board. He requested a cut in salary.

He dug a grave near his Hermitage and for days sat beside it staring into it. On October 24, 1829, the third anniversary of Ann's death, he would write, "God is to me the Great Unknown. I believe in Him, but I find Him not."[19] However, God's power and love did not fail him. He would emerge from the valley of the shadow of death in the strength of his Good Shepherd. He would say of these days, "There is a love that never fails. If I had not felt certain that every additional trial was ordered by infinite love and mercy, I could not have survived my accumulated sufferings."[20]

Adoniram Judson would marry twice more. In 1834 he married Sarah Boardman, a precious and wonderful lady who had lost her missionary husband in death. They were married for eleven years, and she would bear him eight children, five of whom would survive into adulthood. However, she would also die. Then in 1846 he married Emily Chubbuck. They would spend not quite four years together as Adoniram died on April 12, 1850. Emily died four years later in New York of tuberculosis, another slaughtered sheep for her Savior.

We Have His Promise (*Rom. 8:38–39*)

These final verses of Romans 8 constitute what some call "the grand persuasion." Added to the seven items of verse 35 are nine additional realities that have no hope, no chance, of separating the child of God from the love of God found in Christ Jesus our Lord.

Such a promise accompanied Adoniram, who would finish his Burmese translation of the Bible on January 31, 1834. He did a complete revision that was finished in 1840.

Adoniram would live to see about seven thousand people baptized in Burma by the time of his death, and sixty-three congregations were established under 163 missionaries, native pastors, and assistants. Today the Myanmar Baptist Convention has more than 600,000 members in 3,500-plus churches. All of this goes back to the work of God accomplished through the Judsons.

Then there is the matter of the Karen people and the movement of God among them. This in and of itself is a remarkable evidence of the providence of God preparing a particular people for the gospel. Here is the historical record of what occurred.

In the year 1828 an event of vast significance took place. Having come in contact with the Karens, a race of wild people living in remote and almost inaccessible jungles, Judson longed for the opportunity of winning a Karen for Christ and thus reaching his race. This opportunity came to him through Ko Tha Byu, a Karen slave who was sold one day in the bazaar in Moulmein and bought by a native Christian, who forthwith brought him to Judson to be taught and, if possible, evangelized. Ko Tha Byu was a desperate robber bandit. He had taken part in approximately thirty murders and was a hardened criminal with a vicious nature and an ungovernable temper. Patiently, prayerfully, and lovingly, Judson instructed the wretched, depraved creature, who eventually not only yielded to the transforming power of Christ but went through the jungles as a flaming evangelist among his people. The hearts of the Karens had been remarkably and providentially prepared for the reception of the gospel message by a tradition prevalent among them to this effect:

Long, long ago the Karen elder brother and his young white brother lived close together. God gave each of them a Book of Gold containing all they needed for their salvation, success and happiness. The Karen brother neglected and lost his Book of Gold and so he fell into a wretched type of existence, ignorant and cruelly oppressed by the Burmese. The white brother, however, prized his Golden Book, or Book of God, and so, when he sailed away across the oceans, God greatly blessed him. Some day the white brother will return, bringing with him God's Book, which, if the Karen people will receive and obey, will bring to them salvation and untold blessings.

Accordingly, as Ko Tha Byu went on his unwearying preaching tours through the jungles, declaring that the long-looked-for white brother had returned with God's Book, hundreds received the message with gladness.[21]

When a depraved slave, a bandit and murderer, was brought to Judson in 1828, who would have imagined that, a century later, the Christian Karens would have many splendid high schools, hundreds of village schools, some eight hundred self-supporting churches and a Christian constituency of more than 150,000?

Conclusion

On March 4, 1831, Adoniram Judson wrote a letter to his fellow missionary Cephas Bennett, who was a printer, requesting fifteen thousand to twenty thousand tracks. Attending the great annual Buddhist festival at the Shwe Dagon in Rangoon, they experienced a mighty movement of God's Spirit and an increased interest in the gospel. May his words burn deep into our hearts, never to depart:

> [We have distributed] nearly ten thousand tracts, giving to none but those who ask. I presume there have been six thousand applications at the house. Some come two or three months' journey, from the borders of Siam and China—"Sir, we hear that there is an eternal hell. We are afraid of it. Do give us a writing that will tell us how to escape it." Others come from the frontiers of Kathay, a hundred miles north of Ava—"Sir, we have seen a writing that tells about an eternal God. Are you the man that gives away such writings? If so, pray give us one, for we want to know the truth before we die." Others come from the interior of the country, where the name of Jesus Christ is a little known—"Are you Jesus Christ's man? Give us a writing that tells about Jesus Christ."[22]

Jesus Is Everything to Me: Glorious Truth in the Life and Death of Bill Wallace[1]

Philippians 1:21

 William Wallace emerged from relative obscurity to become a national hero. A man of great courage and giftedness, he was tragically cut down in the prime of his life. His people mourned his death. Dedicated to what he believed in, he knowingly and willingly shunned a safer game plan and course of action that would have certainly extended his natural life. Arrested and brutally tortured, beaten and ridiculed, he would die alone with no words of comfort and no one to console him. Much like the apostle Paul in the cold, damp Mamertine dungeon in Rome, he died with no one at his side (2 Tim. 4).

Now, you might find it odd and even out of place that I would dare to draw a comparison between William Wallace of Scotland and the apostle Paul. But then I suspect you probably have the wrong William Wallace in mind, for I am not interested in that William Wallace (of *Braveheart* fame), but William (Bill) Wallace the missionary, a man who served the Chinese people for fifteen years only to be brutally murdered as a martyr on February 10, 1951.

When I think of "Bill Wallace of China," as he is affectionately known, Philippians 1:21 immediately comes to my mind. This is my life verse. Anytime I have the honor of putting my signature in a copy of the Bible, I will append this verse. It is my prayer for my life, my heart's desire in my service for the Lord Jesus. As Paul says in the verse immediately preceding this text, my goal in life is that "Christ will be magnified in my body, whether by life or by death" (Phil. 1:20 NKJV). Bill Wallace of China did both.

For Me to Live Is Christ

Bill Wallace was a Jesus-intoxicated man. For Bill to live was Christ. He proclaimed the gospel of Jesus Christ by word and deed, quietly and without much fanfare to be sure but effectively without question.

Wallace was born in 1908 in Tennessee, the son of a physician. Initially he had little interest in medicine but loved things mechanical including cars and motorcycles. This was providential as it prepared him for a number of unique challenges on the mission field.

At the age of seventeen, while working on a car in the family garage, a nagging question haunted him once again: "What should I do with my life? No, what would God have me do with my life?" Simply, quietly, with a New Testament in his hand, the decisive decision was made: he would be a medical missionary. The date was July 5, 1925. He never looked back or wavered from this commitment.

Wallace would spend the next ten years receiving his education to become a doctor. He would turn down a lucrative offer of a medical practice in the States.

As the time of his medical training drew to a close, a prayer was going up in the ancient China city of Wuchow. Dr. Robert Beddoe needed help at the Stout Memorial Hospital. Writing to the Foreign Mission Board, he pled, "O God, give us a surgeon."[2] At almost the same time, Bill Wallace was penning his own letter to the Foreign Mission Board. Here is what he wrote:

> My name is William L. Wallace and I am now serving as a resident in surgery at Knoxville General Hospital, Knoxville, Tennessee. Since my senior year in high school, I have felt God would have me to be a medical missionary, and to that end I have been preparing myself. I attended the University of Tennessee for my premedical work and received the M.D. from the University Medical School in Memphis. I did an internship here at Knoxville General and remained for a surgical residency.
>
> I am not sure what you desire by way of information, but I am single, twenty-six years old, and I am a member of the Broadway Baptist Church. My mother died when I was eleven and my father, also a physician, passed away two years ago. There were only two of us, and my sister, Ruth Lynn, is planning marriage.
>
> I must confess, I am not a good speaker nor apt as a teacher, but I do feel God can use my training as a physician. As humbly as I know how, I want to volunteer

to serve as a medical missionary under our Southern Baptist Foreign Mission Board. I have always thought of Africa, but I will go anywhere I am needed.[3]

On July 25, 1935, ten years to the month from the time he made his garage commitment and recorded it on the back leaf of his New Testament, Bill was appointed as a medical missionary to Wuchow, South China.

For Bill Wallace, Jesus Christ was everything. Read what this quiet, shy man said to his home church, Broadway Baptist, on September 1, 1935, five weeks after his appointment and just prior to his leaving for China:

I want to express to you my sincere and heartfelt appreciation in making it possible for me to go to China as your missionary, your ambassador for the Lord Jesus Christ . . . You may ask why do I want to go to China . . . and there spend my life and energy. You might say there is much to be done in this country and many have said you can do a lot of good here. Why should I go when there are such hardships and inconveniences? The only answer I have is that it is God's plan that I go.

And God's call was so definite to me. I think he made it definite for me so that there would be no doubt in my mind as to God's plan. So that through the long years of preparation there would be no doubt that I was doing God's will. That has been a comfort and joy to me and I have often thought, "If God can be for me who can be against me."

I want to go because of the needs. And how great is that need! China today is ready and willing to hear and accept the gospel of the Lord Jesus. In Luke 10:2 we

read, "the harvest truly is great, . . . pray ye therefore
. . . that he would send forth laborers into the harvest."
In our mission field today in China and in other countries, hundreds and thousands are going to their death
without knowledge of the Lord Jesus Christ because
we do not have enough missionaries to tell the story.

I want to go to China because someone has prayed
. . . and God heard these prayers and has answered as
he always does when God's people pray. I would rather
be going out as God's missionary this morning than
anything else in the world.

If there is one final word or request that I leave
with you it is this—that you would pray for me, pray
daily that this, your humble servant's ministry and
work might be all that God would have it to be.[4]

Bill Wallace was all about Jesus. This would affect a
number of important decisions in his life. For example, Bill
Wallace would never marry. In 1935 he took a young lady with
him to Ridgecrest, North Carolina. Many expected them to
marry. However, the young lady later said, "[Marriage] was out
of the question. It would have been bigamy; Bill Wallace was
already married to his work!"[5]

To Die Is Gain

China was a boiling cauldron of political instability before
Bill Wallace even arrived. However he was undeterred. Upon
his initial arrival in Wuchow, he was informed that he would
immediately have to return to Hong Kong because of the
unrest. Bill simply and firmly said no. Informed that the captain was upset by his answer and could not be responsible for
his safety, Bill laughed and said, "Tell your captain to rest easy.

He was not responsible for my coming here in the first place, and he doesn't need to be responsible for my staying here!"

Bill would love and serve the Chinese people for fifteen years. His commitment kept him in China through a number of political uprisings, the Japanese invasion of China, World War II, and the Communist takeover of China. On more than a few occasions, he would perform surgery with bombs exploding all around the hospital. Dr. Wallace sent the following letter to his sister; Ruth Wallace Stegall, on September 17, 1938.

> Dear Sister:
>
> Our hospital, our school, and houses were bombed yesterday at 11 a.m. One bomb hit right in middle of hospital and 3 on the side. We are all safe. None of the hospital employees killed. A few hurt. Hospital is full of wounded.
>
> Don't worry. We are all safe. Don't have time to write more.
>
> Don't worry.
>
> William[6]

At one point he was forced to abandon Wuchow but kept the hospital going as he helped move it by boat up the river. This is where his mechanical expertise was especially helpful! Again and again he was urged to leave China, but his response was steadfast, "I will stay as long as I am able to serve."[7] And serve he did.

Once a small child died in his hospital. The parents came. Heartbroken and grieving, he loved and ministered to them. He sat down with them and told them of Jesus and his love for the little children including their own.[8]

During his tenure Dr. Beddoe spoke of a revival that broke out in the hospital since Dr. Wallace's arrival. People were, he said, being healed and saved in Stout Memorial Hospital. He dated the beginning of the Spirit's movement with Bill's arrival.

Read the testimony of his love and ministry to the Chinese people:

> It was while at Fok-Luk that I saw Dr. Wallace refuse his rice allowance and give it to a nurse who was desperately ill with fever. Most of us were sick with diarrhea or fever. Later on I saw him behind the cook tent we had rigged up. He was eating grains of burned rice, hardly palatable, that had been thrown away. When he realized I had seen him, he was terribly embarrassed.
>
> No, he wasn't ashamed of eating that food. No one else would have had it, as hungry as we were. I think he was embarrassed because he did not want me to know how hungry he was.
>
> He was so thin I thought he would blow away if a good wind came along. Somehow, however, he stayed well. He showed us how to eat the bones of what few fowl we found, to get needed vitamins. I believe his unorthodox methods saved all our lives during this period. He was so good, watching over each of us, cheering us, caring for the sick, and doing everything he could to provide for our comfort.
>
> I don't want to offend you, Miss Wright, but we Chinese are not used to seeing Americans or Europeans do things like this. We know the missionaries love us, but there was always a difference. They lived their way and we lived ours, but Dr. Wallace didn't know about the difference. He was one of us. He accepted our portion—all of it.[9]

What Was Said about Bill Wallace?

If you want to find him, find the sickest patient in the hospital, and there he will be.[10]

Bill Wallace was a doctor. His basic ministry was one of healing. But he was in China first of all as a bearer of the good news of Jesus Christ, the glad tidings of forgiveness and eternal life inherent in the old, old message of God's love. Sometimes his soft, stuttering witness to that grace was more effective than the most eloquent evangelist's plea.[11]

Wallace himself said, "With me, it's different. I'm the one to stay. I'm just one piece of man without other responsibilities."[12] Fletcher shows the significance of Wallace's comments by recounting:

One piece of man—it was an old Chinese saying used courteously to depreciate one's value. It indicated a single, unencumbered, expendable person. By it, Bill meant his life was the only one at stake. He was the one thus seated by circumstances, prepared by God for this moment. He was the one to stay on in the face of the unknown, to give the Stout Memorial Hospital and the Baptist witness every chance to continue living, once the Red blight arrived.

"I'm just one piece of man . . . ," Ed Galloway repeated the conversation to his wife as the ferry carried them to Hong Kong. "He really meant it. He has no concept of his own worth and no anxiety for the future that I can see."[13]

And the witness of a Chinese believer concerning their beloved "Waa I Saang," as they called him: "He actually lived before us the life of Christ."[14]

What Was Said by Bill Wallace?

"I am more aware of my limitations than I have ever been. I guess my problem is that I have been imposing my limitations on God."[15]

On returning to China during World War II: "I'm not going back because I'm heroic. Actually, I'm a coward. But I want to go back because it's where I'm supposed to be."[16]

Every effort has been put forth to fulfill the mission of this hospital. The blind receive their sight and the halt and lame walk; the lepers are cleansed; the deaf hear and the poor have the gospel preached to them. It is our hope and prayer that the medical service in this institution shall be on that high plane befitting the glorious gospel which is preached daily within its walls.[17]

Following Pearl Harbor and America's entrance into World War II: "We'll do what God wants us to do. It doesn't make any difference what happens to us. The only important thing is that when it does happen, we be found doing the will of God."[18]

The Superlative Servant of the Savior Goes Home to His Lord

John Piper tells the story of two elderly women, medical missionaries, who died on the mission field serving the Lord Jesus. His pastoral evaluation and assessment are sobering.

As many of you know, Ruby Eliason and Laura Edwards died this week in Cameroon in a car accident—Ruby in her eighties and Laura in her seventies. Ruby gave all her life in medical missions among the poor. Laura, a doctor who practiced in India for many years and then here in the [Twin] Cities, was giving her retirement for the bodies and the souls of the poor in Cameroon. Both died suddenly when their car went over a cliff. Was that a tragedy? Well, in one sense all death is tragic. But consider this. Ruby Eliason and Laura Edwards, at their age, could have been taking it easy here in retirement. Think of tens of thousands of retired people spending their lives in one aimless leisure after another—that is a tragedy. The fact that Jesus Christ took authority to make Ruby Eliason and Laura Edwards valiant for love and truth among the poor and lost and diseased of Cameroon when most Americans are playing their way into eternity—that is not a tragedy. And that he took them suddenly to heaven in their old age in the very moment of their love and service and sacrifice, and without long, drawn-out illnesses and without protracted and oppressive feelings of uselessness—that is not a tragedy. Rather, I say, "Give me that death, O Jesus Christ, Lord of the universe, give me that life and that ministry and that death!"[19]

The death of another medical missionary is of a similar, but not identical, nature.

On December 18, 1950, Bill Wallace completed an exhaustive day at Stout Memorial. Communist activities had been on the increase, and many missionaries had been evacuated from their field assignment. Bill Wallace chose to stay and serve. Early December 19, before dawn, Chinese Communists lied their way into the clinic grounds of the hospital. Chinese soldiers ordered Bill Wallace and other workers out of their bedrooms and led them to the hospital proper. Immediately the soldiers began to accuse Dr. Wallace of being an American spy in an attempt to discredit him before the Chinese people who so deeply loved and respected him. Calmly and clearly Bill Wallace responded to their accusations by saying, "We are what we seem to be. We are doctors and nurses and hospital staff engaged in healing the suffering and sick in the name of Jesus Christ. We are here for no other reason."[20] The soldiers went to Bill's room and returned with a small handgun. There is no question it had been planted after Bill was forced to leave his bedroom. There is no historical evidence that Bill ever owned or shot a gun in his life. However, the Communists had what they wanted. He was arrested and his nurse assistant Everley Hayes placed under house arrest. What follows is the sad and courageous account of Bill's final days from biographer Jesse Fletcher:

> Faced with wild charges of espionage, Bill was placed in a cell and left alone for some time. He was able to receive meals from the hospital and had an opportunity to tell his jailer of Jesus Christ and to preach from a cell window to two or three peasants who gathered to hear him.
>
> A week after his arrest, the Communists turned away the man who brought Bill's food one morning. They said he would no longer be able to receive it. That night a called meeting was held at one of the big town halls in Wuchow and all citizens of any importance were commanded to attend. There the man who had arrested the doctor arose to inform the crowd that Dr. William Wallace of the Stout Memorial Hospital had confessed to being a spy. They spoke of the gun and hinted at dark deeds the doctor had done. They asked

for those who had any accusation against Dr. Wallace to come forward with their charges. None came.

What the Communists had secured from Bill was a statement concerning his name, age, length of service in China, and other factual matters. Reading it and realizing it was all true, he signed it. The Communists then typed into a blank part of the paper the statement that he had been sent to China as a secret service man by the United States government. This was the confession.

The next day, Bill was awakened early and shoved out into a courtyard where he realized for the first time he was not the only missionary being held. He recognized a Catholic sister and a bishop.

A placard with obscene and derisive accusations and charges was placed over him, and his hands were tied behind his back. With others, he was marched through the streets to the Fu River and across to the main prison halfway up the hill—that same hill to which he had gone so many times before for fellowship with his friends, the Christian and Missionary Alliance people. On the way over, shoved by a guard, he fell and badly hurt a hand that he threw out to break his fall. He received no care.

Daily, sometimes hourly, often through the night at the prison, he was awakened and brought to an interrogator's room. The world had yet to hear of brainwashing, which was to be more fully publicized after the release of the prisoners of the Korean War, but Bill Wallace began to experience it the second week of his imprisonment.

Their accusations, viciously and vehemently proclaimed, bewildered and upset him. They were shouted over and over again, growing in intensity, growing in degradation, allowing for no defense. No excuses or answers were permitted. It overwhelmed him to hear accusations of incompetence in surgery, of murdering and maiming Chinese patients, of performing illegal and obscene operations. His interrogators hinted that doctors from all over China had gathered evidence on him and were demanding his punishment. When exhausted, he was returned to the cell—a bare room with a thin pallet for protection from the damp and cold and filth of the floor.

On another day, all the foreign prisoners were gathered into an open courtyard and one by one forced to stand by a table piled high with guns, bullets, opium, radios, and other items supposed to have been confiscated in the raids in which they were arrested. Then each one was photographed behind the table. When it came Bill's turn to step up to the table, he was almost pushed into it by the guard behind him. Rudely, he was posed, with great stress being put upon his holding the aerial of a radio—to prove the spying charges.

It was obvious to the Catholic missionaries who were in prison with Bill and who were later released, that he was shaken and strained by the ordeal of interrogation. The rest of that day the prisoners were sport for a large crowd of Communist soldiers, men and women, and they suffered numerous brutalities. Toward the end of the day, one of the missionaries found an opportunity to inquire of Bill how he was holding out. With a tender smile, he replied, "All right, trusting in the Lord."

From his cell in the night, Bill sometimes cried out in agony after the battle was over. With pieces of paper and a smuggled pencil, he wrote short affirmations to try to keep his mind centered on things that he could anchor himself to. Some were Scripture passages, others simple denials of guilt, protests of innocence. He stuck these on the walls of his barren room and repeated them to himself in an effort to prepare for the next interrogation.

But each one came like a high wave. At times, he was all but overwhelmed by the interrogation. Delirium, crying, and blank periods came, but he fought on—clinging to his faith. His fellow victims, not yet subjected to the intensive brainwashing, helplessly watched this inhuman assault on one of the greatest men they had ever known. Frantically, they tried to reach him from time to time by calling through their cells. But it was a lonely battle which only Bill and the Lord—who loved him and who, somehow, in his wildest delirium he affirmed—could face.

Then something went wrong. The Communists plainly intended to brainwash their victim into an open confession, to have him repudiate publicly all that he was and all he had stood for. They thought their goal was within reach, but the tough spirit would not capitulate so easily, and his protests rang through the night.

The guards, driven by fear or perhaps guilt, came to his cell in the night with long poles and cruelly thrust them between the cell bars to jab the doctor into unconsciousness. Somebody figured wrong. For that one night the battle came to an end, and, though no one heard Bill Wallace cry, "It is finished," he offered up his spirit and brought his ministry and mission to a close. Quietly, his soul slipped from his torn body and his exhausted mind and went to be with the One he had so faithfully and resolutely served.

Bill Wallace was dead to the world, but alive forever with God.

The next morning the guards ran down the cell-block, crying that the doctor had hanged himself. Asking the two Catholic fathers imprisoned in the cell to come with them, they went into the cell where the body of the doctor was hanging from a beam by a rope of braided quilt. The guards tried to get the fathers to sign a statement that he had committed suicide. They would not do so.

Back at the hospital where the staff had waited prayerfully through all these weeks, word came to go and get the body of Dr. Wallace. Everley went with her servant and another nurse. They would not let her go into the cell, but they let the servant in, and Everley instructed him quietly to be sure to note the character-istics of the body. The facial characteristics of hanging were missing—bulging eyes, discolored face, swollen tongue. Instead, the upper torso was horribly bruised.

A cheap wooden coffin had been brought, and as soon as the body was dressed, it was put into the coffin and nailed shut by the Communist soldiers.[21]

Bill Wallace was dead. He was just forty-three years old.

Conclusion

Bill Wallace died on February 10, 1951. Those who worked close beside him were not allowed to see his body as the Communists attempted to hide their brutal torture of this precious servant to the Chinese people and King Jesus. Our nation was outraged, and God's people wept all over the world. Immediately testimonies to this faithful missionary began to pop up.

A letter from Dr. Theron Rankin, executive secretary of the Foreign Mission Board:

When God chooses someone to make a superlative witness of His love, He chooses a superlative child of His. He chose His own Son, Jesus, to make the witness on the Cross. And now it seems that He chose Bill to make this witness. To give his life in love and service for the people whom he served fits in naturally and harmoniously with Bill's life. The two things go together because he was that kind of man. His life's service among men bears out the testimony of his death. Bill's death was not the result of his being caught by a situation from which he could not escape. He deliberately chose his course with a committal that made him ready to take any consequences that might come.[22]

From Dr. Baker James Cauthen, at the time Dr. Wallace's regional leader:

Many things about the death of Bill Wallace make us think of the death of the Christ. The authorities were envious of his place in the hearts of people. They used falsehood in order to bring charges against him. They tried to represent him as an agent of the American government, as the Jews tried to represent Jesus as one stirring up revolt against Rome. They sought to stir up public sentiment by calling large groups of people together. They subjected him to a bitter and cruel imprisonment.

Just as in the case of Jesus the enemies of the truth sought to discredit His testimony by declaring the disciples had come and stolen away His body, so in Wuchow the Communists stated that Dr. Wallace had died by strangling himself. This nobody believes even a moment.[23]

By God's grace the life of this servant of the Lord Jesus has not been forgotten. There is a wonderful biography by Jesse Fletcher entitled *Bill Wallace of China*. It has been referred to throughout this chapter. A motion picture based on the book was produced.[24] In Puchan, Korea, there is the Wallace Memorial Hospital. The Baptist Student Union at the University of Tennessee Medical Center is named for Bill Wallace. In Knoxville there is also the vibrant and growing Wallace Memorial Baptist Church.[25] However, the real memorial to this man is not in buildings but in the hundreds of men and women who have been inspired by his life to go to the nations as missionaries for our Lord.

On January 12, 1985, a service was held at the Wallace Memorial Baptist Church as the remains of William Lindsey Wallace were returned and laid to rest in the place where he grew up. In that service Dr. James McCluskey powerfully noted:

I cannot imagine that this congregation of believers called Wallace Memorial Baptist Church, would today have the same missions concern, outreach, love, fellowship, and joy if it was known by any other name than Wallace Memorial.

I know that the remains of William Lindsey Wallace live on in my own life, motivating and challenging me after these more than twenty-five years as pastor of this church named in his memory.

The remains of William Lindsey Wallace are going to Costa Rica tomorrow in the life and ministry of Patricia Stooksbury as she returns there to continue her missionary service. Pat felt God's call to missions

and responded to that call in the missionary environ-
ment of a church called Wallace Memorial.

The remains of William Lindsey Wallace are in
Grenada, West Indies, today as Charlotte and Carter
Davis serve there. They experienced a call and
response to serve in a spirit of missions concern culti-
vated in this church.

The remains of William Lindsey Wallace are in
Ecuador today where Dale Maddox is completing his
second year as a missionary journeyman. His missions
experience came as a member of a youth missions
team sent out by Wallace Memorial Baptist Church.

The remains of William Lindsey Wallace are in
the lives of more than twenty-five young people of this
church who are today either serving or preparing to serve
in church-related vocations and in the lives of thousands
of others who have been inspired and led by his life. The
remains of William Lindsey Wallace are scattered today
into the uttermost parts of the earth where missionaries
give witness that Jesus Christ is Lord.[26]

There was no funeral service for Bill Wallace. The
government officials would not allow it. A grave was dug, and
a nailed-shut coffin was lowered into the ground. The soldiers
stayed until the burial was complete, and then they drove
everyone away from this lonely, unmarked grave. However,
it did not stay unmarked. Despite danger to themselves,
friends of the kind, brave doctor collected funds for a marker
and lovingly built a small monument over the solitary grave.
Inscribed were seven single words that accurately captured this
superlative servant of our Savior: "For to me to live is Christ."
And we know the rest of the story: "To die is gain."

CHAPTER 4

The Power of a Consecrated Life: The Ministry of Lottie Moon[1]

Romans 12:1

 Lottie Moon was born Charlotte (Lottie) Diggs Moon on December 12, 1840, in Albemarle County, Virginia. She entered the world as a part of Southern aristocracy prior to the Civil War, a war that would devastate her family's fortunes. Her family's wealth was one-fortieth of its prewar value after the war ended. She would die on December 24, 1912, aboard a ship in the Japanese harbor of Kōbe. She was frail, weak, and nearly starved, having just passed her seventy-second birthday. She weighed no more than fifty pounds.[2]

Lottie served our Lord for thirty-nine years on the mission field, mostly in China. Best estimates say this mighty little woman towered all of four feet, three inches. It was never said that she was beautiful, but this little lady had a

47

certain attractiveness about her and a powerful personality that would be essential in her service on the mission field. She taught in schools for girls and made many evangelistic trips into China's interior to share the gospel with women and girls. She would even preach, against her wishes, to men because then as now there were not enough men on the mission field.

I have no doubt, having spent many months in her biography and letters, that Miss Lottie would be both amazed and embarrassed at all the fuss that is made about her each year by Southern Baptists. She knew that in 1888 Southern Baptists, at her request, raised $3,315 to send three new female missionaries to China. She could never have imagined that in 2006, $150,178,098.06 was raised in her name. Since the inception of the Lottie Moon Christmas Offering, $2.8 billion has been raised for missions in her name. More than half of the International Mission Board's 2008 budget comes from the offering that honors her name.

Here is the power of a consecrated life, a life sold out to the lordship of Christ, a life our Lord sovereignly chose to multiply many times over. This is the life we see outlined by the apostle Paul in Romans 12:1. Having spent eleven chapters explaining sin and salvation, sanctification and sovereignty, he now moves on that basis to address service and what I call "the consecrated life."

Such a life is seen in Lottie Moon. Hers was not a perfect life, no doubt. It was, however, a powerful life, a life lived for King Jesus and a life worthy of our careful study and attention.

Four marvelous truths emerge from this text that find a beautiful echo in the life of Lottie Moon, an echo I pray will find its sound in my life and yours.

Live a Grateful Life

Paul encourages us by the mercies of God, a shorthand for the many blessings he has unpacked for us in Romans 1–11. Gratitude should overwhelm every man or woman who has grasped the magnitude of sin and the majesty of salvation. Accepted in Christ by my heavenly Father, I live a life of gratitude for all he has done for me. No request is deemed out of bounds or too great.

Lottie came to this conviction but not until she was in college. When Lottie was a child, her mother read to her and her siblings the Bible and other religious books. One was the story of Ann Judson, the wife of Adoniram Judson and the first Baptist woman missionary from America. In December 1858, at the age of eighteen, Lottie placed her faith and trust in Jesus. The preacher was the famous Baptist leader John Broadus. He would also baptize her and encourage her in her service to our Lord. In fact, Broadus's challenge to missions planted the seed for foreign service in her heart, though at the time a single woman going to the nations was unthinkable.

This grateful life was born of a confidence in the providence and sovereignty of God. She wrote, "I do not believe that any trouble comes upon us unless it is needed, and it seems to me that we ought to be just as thankful for sorrow as for joys."[3] She would oft recall Broadus's prayer, "Send us affliction and trouble, blight our dearest hopes if need be, that we may learn more fully to depend on Thee."[4]

And later in a letter to J. C. Williams, February 25, 1876, she wrote: "But the work is God's and we do not fear the final results. 'The heathen shall be given to His Son for His inheritance,' and we must be content to await His own time."[5]

Thus gratitude, growing trust in divine providence, colored Lottie's perspective on life. She needed this. When she was twelve, her wealthy father died of a heart attack or stroke while on a business trip. Lottie's mother, Anna-Maria Moon, assumed family leadership.

While on the field famine raged in north China as Lottie returned there in December 1877. She and other missionaries gave to relief programs and shared personally as they could to relieve the suffering.

Early in 1878 Lottie opened a girls' boarding school for higher-class Chinese. Her purpose was evangelistic. She knew the school would help her enter pupils' homes since the exclusive citizens of Tengchow wanted little to do with "foreign devils," as the missionaries were often called, otherwise. God also accomplished other noble purposes.

She managed to save about a third of her pupils from the practice of binding girls' feet. The custom usually began about the time a girl would be entering school. The four small toes were bent under and bandaged and drawn toward the heel until bones broke. The suffering young women wound up with a three-inch foot and a pointed big toe. Often infection, illness, and even death resulted. God was at work in surprising ways.

Lottie's life was often a life of extended loneliness. Many times she would be the only Southern Baptist missionary in northern China. Her lone companion was her Lord. But she stayed with the work God had for her. She relocated to P'ingtu in December 1885. Aided by a Chinese couple from Tengchow, she rented a four-room, dirt-floor house for $24 a year, planning to stay until summer. She ate and lived as the Chinese did. No one she knew spoke English.

She quickly adapted to the local dialect. She began visiting surrounding villages and within a few months had made 122 trips to thirty-three different places. She gratefully trusted our Lord in trying and difficult circumstances.

Her gratitude to God was also the basis of her challenge to folks back home to give to the work of missions. She opposed raising funds by entertainments or gimmicks. She wrote:

> I wonder how many of us really believe that it is more blessed to give than to receive. A woman who accepts that statement of our Lord Jesus Christ as a fact and not as "impractical idealism," will make giving a principle of her life. She will lay aside sacredly not less than one-tenth of her income or her earnings as the Lord's money, which she would no more dare touch for personal use than she would steal. How many there are among our women, alas, who imagine that because "Jesus paid it all," they need pay nothing, forgetting that the prime object of their salvation was that they should follow in the footsteps of Jesus Christ![6]

Persecution broke out against Christians in Sha-ling in 1890. Relatives of one of the first inquirers, Dan Ho Bang, tied him to a pole and beat him, but he refused to worship at ancestral tablets. A young convert, Li Show-ting, was beaten by his brothers, who tore out his hair; still, he remained steadfast in his faith. He was to become the great evangelist of north China, baptizing more than ten thousand believers.

Lottie rushed to Sha-ling and told the persecution leaders, "If you attempt to destroy his church, you will have to kill me first. Jesus gave Himself for us Christians. Now I am ready to die for Him."[7] One of the mob prepared to kill her but was restrained. Lottie calmed the terrified believers and remained with them until the persecution waned. When the believers did not retaliate with the usual legal action, the Chinese grew in their respect of Christians and asked to hear of the new faith. The church became the strongest in north China, with its members evangelizing in nearby villages.

Let me offer one final example of her confidence in the God of providence. China's revolution broke out late in 1911. Fighting was intense around Baptist mission stations in north China. The U.S. consul asked missionaries in Hwanghsien to move to a safer port city, and they agreed—all but Lottie. When she learned Chinese hospital personnel had been left alone in Hwanghsien, she made her way safely through warring troops and took charge of the hospital, encouraging the terrified nurses and other personnel by her courage.

They resumed work, caring for the ill and wounded. When Dr. Ayers and other male missionaries risked their lives to return, they were amazed to find Lottie directing the hospital quite efficiently, as she had done for ten days.

With the hospital in rightful hands, Lottie packed to return home.

Live a Total Life

The Bible calls us to "present our bodies." This is a personal and individual decision we all must make. It is volitional. It is to be total. "All of you, all of the time" captures the thrust of Paul's challenge. Once she came to Christ, Lottie Moon made such an agenda her life's calling and commitment.

In college she mastered Greek, Hebrew, Latin, Italian, French, and Spanish. In 1861 she graduated from Albemarle Female Institute, counterpart to the University of Virginia, one of the first women in the South to receive a master's degree. Broadus would call her "the most educated (or cultured) woman in the South."[8]

During the Civil War she and her sisters Colie and Mollie nursed soldiers at Charlottesville as well as her brother Orie back home.

Prior to leaving for China, she taught Sunday School near Viewpoint to both black and white children.

Lottie felt her call to China "as clear as a bell" in February 1873, after hearing a sermon on missions at First Baptist Church in Cartersville, Georgia.[9] Lottie left the service to go to her room, where she prayed all afternoon.

On July 7, 1873, the Foreign Mission Board appointed Charlotte Digges Moon as a missionary. She was asked to join her sister who actually had preceded her to the mission field in Tengchow. About to sail from San Francisco, Lottie received word that Baptist women in Cartersville would support her. There was no Cooperative Program at this time. It would not come into existence until 1925!

In village after village she would travel to speak from early morning to late evening, from the kang, on the street, in the yard of dirty homes, traveling in shentzes or riding donkeys, in the heat and dust of summer or wintry rain and snow. She was constantly in contact with the people, continually at risk of exposure to smallpox and other diseases. Yet she suppressed her craving for cultured life and conversation and her Southern tastes—all for the cause of Christ. "As I wander from village to village," she said, "I feel it is no idle fancy that the Master walks beside me, and I hear His voice saying gently, 'I am with you always, even unto the end.'"[10]

She found strength in prayer and Bible reading and in devotional classics. She often wrote quotations from spiritual writings in the margin of her Bible or devotional books. One favorite was from Francis de Sales: "Go on joyously as much as you can, and if you do not always go on joyously, at best go on courageously and confidently."[11]

Lottie suggested to Dr. H. A. Tupper, head of the Mission Board, that the board follow the pattern of some other mission groups and provide for a year of furlough after ten years on the field. The board eventually adopted such a policy but not until several missionaries in China died prematurely and others returned home in broken health.

Lottie repeatedly struggled with the tragic fact that more did not answer the call to missions, especially men. What follows are the texts of letters she wrote to Tupper and others of the need (all letters are addressed to Tupper unless otherwise noted):

November 1, 1873:

What we need in China is more workers. The harvest is very great, the laborers, oh! so few. Why does the Southern Baptist church lag behind in this great work? . . . I think your idea is correct, that a young man should ask himself not if it is his duty to go to the heathen, but if he may dare stay at home. The command is so plain: "Go."[12]

April 27, 1874:

Oh that we had active and zealous men who would go far and wide scattering books and tracts and preaching the word to the vast multitudes of this land.[13]

November 4, 1875:

I write today moved by feelings which come over me constantly when I go out on country trips. "The harvest is plenteous, the laborers are few." . . . What we find missionaries can do in the way of preaching the gospel even in the immediate neighborhood of this city, is but as the thousandth part of a drop in the bucket compared with what should be done. I do not pretend to aver that there is any spiritual interest among the people. They literally "sit in darkness & in the shadow of death." The burden of our words to them is the folly and sin of idol worship. We are but doing pioneer work, but breaking up the soil in which we believe others shall sow a bountiful crop. But, as in the natural soil, four or five laborers cannot possibly cultivate a radius of twenty miles, so cannot we, a mission of five people, do more than make a beginning of what should be done. . . . But is there no way to arouse the churches on this subject? We missionaries find it in our hearts to say to them in all humility, "Now then we are ambassadors for Christ; as though God did beseech you by us, we pray you, in Christ's stead," to remember the heathen. We implore you to send us help. Let not these heathen sink down into eternal death without one opportunity to hear that blessed Gospel which is to you the source of all joy and comfort. The work that constantly presses upon us is greater than time or strength permit us to do.[14]

April 14, 1876:

There was a large crowd pretty soon in attendance, so many that the hall would not hold them & they adjourned to the yard. I hope you won't think me desperately unfeminine, but I spoke to them all, men, women, and children, pleading with them to turn from their idolatry to the True and Living God. I

should not have dared to remain silent with so many
souls before me sunk in heathen darkness.[15]

October 10, 1878:

Odd that with five hundred Baptist preachers in
the state of Virginia we must rely on a Presbyterian
minister to fill a Baptist pulpit. I wonder how these
things look in Heaven: they certainly look very queer
in China. But then we Baptists are a great people
as we never tire of saying at our associations and
Conventions, & possibly our way of doing things is the
best![16]

November 11, 1878:

But how inadequate our force! Here is a province
of thirty million souls & Southern Baptists can only
send one man & three women to tell them the story
of redeeming love. Oh! That my words could be as a
trumpet call stirring the hearts of my brethren and
sisters to pray, to labor, to give themselves to this people. "But," some will say, "we must have results, else
interest flags." I have seen the husbandman go forth in
the autumn to plow the fields; later, I have seen him
scatter the seed broadcast; anon, the tiny green shoots
came up scarcely visible at first; then the snows of
winter fell concealing them for weeks; spring brought
its fructifying rains, its genial sunshine, and lo! in June
the golden harvest. We are now, a very, very few feeble
workers, scattering the grain broadcast according as
time and strength permit. God will give the harvest;
doubt it not. But the laborers are so few. Where we

have four, we should have not less than one hundred.
Are these wild words? They would not seem so were
the church of God awake to her high privileges & her
weighty responsibilities."[17]

An "Open Letter" to the *Religious Herald*, no date:

I am trying honestly to do the work that could fill the
hands of three or four women, and in addition must
do much work that ought to be done by young men.
. . . Our dilemma—to do men's work or to sit silent
at religious services conducted by men just emerging
from heathenism.[18]

January 8, 1889:

There is so much work to be done, too, that ought to
be done by men. A young woman could not do the
work & retain the respect of Chinese men. . . . While
I do not a little for the men & the boys, I do not feel
bound to stay on their account. Still, I must add that
the work is suffering and will continue to suffer in that
department for want of a man living on the spot.[19]

September 1877, to the *Foreign Mission Journal*:

In the vast continent of Africa, we have one white
missionary and one colored. In Japan we have—not
one. In China we have at present eight missionaries.
Putting the population of China at four hundred million, this gives one missionary for fifty million people.
Yet, we call ourselves Missionary Baptists.

Our Lord says, "Go ye into all the world & preach the gospel to every creature." Are we obeying this command?"[20]

January 1888, to the *Foreign Mission Journal*:

The needs of these people press upon my soul, and I cannot be silent. It is grievous to think of these human souls going down to death without even one opportunity of hearing the name of Jesus. People talk vaguely about the heathen, picturing them as scarcely human, or at best, as ignorant barbarians. If they could live among them as I do, they would find in the men much to respect and admire; in the women and girls they would see many sweet and loving traits of character. They would feel, pressing upon their heart and conscience, the duty of giving the gospel to them. It does seem strange that when men and women can be found willing to risk life—or, at least, health and strength— in order that these people may hear the gospel, that Christians withhold the means to send them. Once more I urge upon the consciences of my Christian brethren and sisters the claims of these people among whom I dwell. Here I am working alone in a city of many thousand inhabitants, with numberless villages clustered around or stretching away in the illuminate distance: how many can I reach?

It fills one with sorrow to see these people so earnest in their worship of false gods, seeking to work out their salvation by supposed works of merit, with no one to tell them of a better way. Then, to remember the wealth hoarded in Christian coffers! The money lavished on fine dresses and costly living! Is it not time

for Christian men and women to return to the simplicity of earlier times? Should we not press it home upon
our consciences that the sole object of our conversion
was not the salvation of our own souls, but that we
might become co-workers with our Lord and Master
in the conversion of the world?[21]

May 1889 to the *Foreign Mission Journal*:

One cannot help asking sadly, why is love of gold more
potent than love of souls? The number of men mining
and prospecting for gold in Shantung is more than double the number of men representing Southern Baptists!
What a lesson for Southern Baptists to ponder![22]

Live a Sacrificial Life

"A living sacrifice." The phrase sounds odd, oxymoronic.
And yet is its meaning not plain? The consecrated life is both
alive and dead at the same time. When I am sold out to Christ,
there are times in which I am active, vibrant, alive. Since I am
sold out to Christ, there are some things that once thrilled me,
delighted me, and consumed me; but I am now dead to them.
I know them but I am dead to them. They are not my life, my
passion, any longer. It is now all about Christ and his calling
upon my life. Such a life the Bible says is holy and acceptable
to God.

The little aristocratic lady from Virginia lived such a life
on many levels. Listen to her spirited correspondence to Dr.
Tupper, dated November 11, 1878, concerning living conditions on the field:

Possibly you may have noticed throughout this letter that I have made frequent illusions to physical

discomforts & to weariness of mind & body. I have
always been ashamed in writing of missionary work
to dwell upon physical hardships & then too we get
so accustomed to take them as a matter of course
that it does not occur to us to speak of them save in a
general way. In this letter I have purposely departed
from my usual reticence upon such matters because
I know that there are some who, in their pleasant
homes in America, without any real knowledge of
the facts, declare that the days of missionary hardships are over. To speak in the open air, in a foreign
tongue, from six to eleven times a day, is no trifle.
The fatigue of travel is something. The inns are simply the acme of discomfort. If anyone fancies that
sleeping on brick beds, in rooms with dirt floor, with
walls blackened by the smoke of generations—the
yard to these quarters being also the stable yard, &
the stable itself being in three feet of the door of your
apartment—if anyone thinks all this agreeable, then I
wish to declare most emphatically that as a matter of
taste I differ. If anyone thinks he would like this constant contact with what an English writer has called
the "Great Unwashed," I must still say that from
experience I find it unpleasant. If anyone thinks that
constant exposure to the risk of small-pox and other
contagious diseases against which the Chinese take
no precautions whatever, is just the most charming
thing in life, I must still beg leave to say that I shall
continue to differ in opinion. In a word, let him come
out and try it. A few days roughing it as we ladies do
habitually will convince the most skeptical. There is a
passage from Farrar's "Life of Christ," which recurred
forcibly to my mind during this recent country tour.

"From early dawn . . . to late evening in whatever house He had selected for His nightly rest, the multitude came crowding about him, not respecting his privacy, not allowing for his weariness, eager to see Him. . . . There was no time even to eat bread. Such a life is not only to the last degree trying and fatiguing, but to a refined and high strung nature. . . . This incessant publicity, this apparently illimitable toil becomes simply maddening unless the spirit be sustained." He was the Son of God but we missionaries, we are only trying in a very poor way to walk in His footsteps & this "boundless sympathy and love" is of the divine and not the human.

A few words more and I have done. We are astonished at the wide door opened us for work. We have such access to the people, to their hearts & homes as we could not have dared to hope two years ago.[23]

But there is one living sacrifice Lottie made that I especially wish to draw to your attention. Miss Moon never married, though she did receive a proposal that she would turn down. There was a brilliant Hebrew and Old Testament scholar named Crawford Toy. Some have called him the "crown jewel" of Southern Seminary as he was one of its earliest and, without question, brightest young faculty members. Though all of the precise details are not clear, a general outline of the relationship between Dr. Toy and Miss Moon can be sketched.

They met when she was a student at Albemarle Female Institute and he was an assistant to the principal, a noted educator name John Hart. At the time Lottie "was considered a brain and a heretic."[24] It appears Lottie and Crawford developed something more than a student-pupil relationship during her time there.

Toy committed himself to be a missionary. Lottie would make the same commitment a few years later. Set to sail for the mission field in 1860, Toy mysteriously did not go.

In 1870 Toy returned from studying in Germany to teach at Southern Seminary. He had ingested the liberal historical criticism popular in European universities.

Around 1876 Lottie returned from China accompanying her sister Edmonia ("Eddie") who had suffered an emotional breakdown while on the field. At this time she and Crawford Toy saw each other and apparently rekindled their relationship. This would continue in some measure until 1882.

Controversy on the mission field led Lottie to consider leaving China and returning to America to marry Toy. Some Moon scholars believe the proposed marriage may have occurred earlier when Toy was planning to go to Japan and Lottie was beginning to sense God's call to missions as well.

The wedding never took place. According to Toy's own family, the engagement was broken because of religious differences. It appears Toy's slide into theological liberalism and backtracking on going to the mission field led Lottie to break off their engagement. Toy would go to Harvard and die a Unitarian. Lottie would remain in China and die alone. Lottie was later asked by a young relative, "Aunt Lottie, have you ever been in love?" She answered, "Yes, but God had first claim on my life, and since the two conflicted, there could be no question about the results."[25]

In 1888 Lottie would forcibly address the "new theology" of Toy and others that was being much discussed in America. With keen insight she saw it would be fatal to the mission enterprise. She used the occasion to critique its danger and chide her fellow Baptists for their missionary indifference.

Her biographer Catherine Allen summarizes her prophetic call:

> Although she was committed primarily to teaching the women, and next to dealing with the children, she could not keep the men from listening from adjoining rooms. In the case of Sha-ling, the men were the primary inquirers. Each evening and on Sunday she would conduct a service of worship. In a little low-ceilinged room, lit by wicks in saucers of bean oil, the worshipers would gather. A makeshift screen of grain stalks divided the crown of men from women. With Miss Moon's direction, the semi-heathen men would lead singing, read Scripture, rehearse the catechism, and pray. Miss Moon would sometimes comment on the Scripture. If Mrs. Crawford were present, she would be willing to deliver what amounted to a sermon.
>
> With such ready response to the gospel, Miss Moon was incredulous that Southern Baptist preachers and young women were not flocking to China. From Pingtu she quickened the flow of appeals. Now she turned to shaming, chiding, flattering—any tactic to get the attention of the apathetic Baptists. In one appeal she concluded that the folks back home had all adopted the "new theology" the Baptist editors had been criticizing ever since the Toy episode. One had predicted that "new theology" would quench the missionary spirit.
>
> 'I conclude that the large majority of Southern Baptists have adopted this 'new theology,'" she wrote. "Else, why this strange indifferences to missions? Why these scant contributions. . . . The needs of these

people press upon my soul, and I cannot be silent. People talk vaguely about the heathen, picturing them as scarcely human, or at best, as ignorant barbarians. If they could live among them as I do, they would find in the men much to respect and admire; in the women and girls they would see many sweet and loveable traits of character. . . . Here I am working alone in a city of many thousand inhabitants with numberless villages. How many can I reach?"[26]

Live a Worshipful Life

The consecrated life is what Paul calls "your reasonable service" (Rom. 12:1 NKJV). Other English translations render it "your spiritual act of worship" (NIV); "your spiritual service of worship" (NASB); "your spiritual worship" (ESV and HCSB).

Paul's point is that a consecrated life is a worshipping life. It is a constant and continuous life of service lived out twenty-four hours a day, seven days a week in thanksgiving for all that we enjoy in Christ. It is a life truly satisfied in God, his good, his glory. Such satisfaction is evidence in Lottie's life.

In her Bible Lottie wrote, "Words fail to express my love for this holy Book, my gratitude for its author, for his love and goodness. How shall I thank him for it?"[27]

Lottie also had a great confidence in the sovereignty of God and a dependence on the work of the Holy Spirit. She said, "I have a firm conviction that I am immortal 'til my work is done."[28] She also wrote, "I feel my weakness and inability to accomplish anything without the aid of the Holy Spirit. Make special prayer for the outpouring of the Holy Spirit in P'ingtu, that I may be clothed with power from on high by the indwelling of the Spirit in my heart."[29]

She further had a great love for the lost, which propelled her on in this worshipful life she lived. She said, "We must go out and live among them, manifesting the gentle, loving spirit of our Lord. We need to make friends before we can hope to make converts."[30]

During the 1890s Lottie set a goal to visit two hundred villages every three months. She would write, "I have never found mission work more enjoyable. . . . I constantly thank God. He has given me a work I love so much."[31]

As an aside, Lottie adopted traditional Chinese dress and learned their customs. Not only did she serve them, she identified with them, even in her death. The following letter was printed in the August 1887 *Foreign Mission Journal*:

> I feel that I would gladly give my life to working among such a people and regard it as a joy and privilege. Yet, to women who may think of coming, I would say, count well the cost. You must give up all that you hold dear, and live a life that is, outside of your work, narrow and contracted to the last degree. If you really love the work, it will atone for all you give up, and when your work is ended and you go Home, to see the Master's smile and hear his voice of welcome will more than repay your toils amid the heathen.[32]

In the year of her death, 2,358 persons were baptized in her field of service, nearly doubling the Baptist population in the area.[33]

Her worshipful life also grew out of a tremendous love for Jesus.

In a May 10, 1879, letter to Tupper, she wrote:

> Recall for a moment the thoughts that crowd upon the mind. This ancient continent of Asia whose soil

you are treading was the chosen theatre for the advent of the Son of God. In a rush of grateful emotion there came to your mind the lines of that grand old hymn the "Dies Irae," "Seeking me Thy worn feet hasted, On the cross Thy soul death tasted," and your heart is all aglow with longing to bear to others the priceless gift that you have received, that thus you may manifest your thankfulness and love to the giver. He "went about doing good"; in a humble manner you are trying to walk in his footsteps. As you wend your way from village to village, you feel it is no idle fancy that the Master walks beside you and you hear his voice saying gently, "Lo! I am with you always even unto the end." And the soul makes answer in the words of St. Bernard, that holy man of God, "Lord Jesus, thou are home and friends and fatherland to me." Is it any wonder that as you draw near to the villages a feeling of exultation comes over you? That your heart goes up to God in glad thanksgiving that he has so trusted you as to commit to your hands this glorious gospel that you may convey its blessings to those who still sit in darkness? When the heart is full of such joy, it is no effort to speak to the people: you could not keep silent if you would. Mere physical hardships sink into merited insignificance. What does one care for comfortless inns, hard beds, hard fare, when all around is a world of joy and glory and beauty?[34]

On her deathbed, speaking to her friend and fellow missionary Cynthia Miller, Lottie said: "Jesus is here right now. You can pray now that he will fill my heart and stay with me. For when Jesus comes in, he drives out all evil. . . . Jesus loves me. This I know, for the Bible tells me so. Little ones to him belong. They are weak, but he is strong. Do you know this song, Miss Miller?"[35]

Miss Miller would write following Lottie's death, "It is infinitely touching that those who work hardest and make the most sacrifices for the Master should suffer because those in the homeland fail to give what is needed."[36]

Dr. T. W. Ayers said, "[Lottie Moon] is one woman who will have her crown covered with stars. She is one of the most unselfish saints God ever made."[37]

Conclusion

Lottie Moon died at age seventy-two, a frail fifty pounds. She had stopped eating due to illness and concern over famine conditions.[38] Her remains were cremated at Yokohama, Japan, on December 26. Personal effects consisted of one steamer trunk. The executor of her estate sold all of her personal property and cleared her bank account of $254 in inflated local currency. He wrote with a broken heart, "The heiress of Viewmount did not have enough estate to pay her way back to Virginia."[39] She had given all she had to King Jesus. Twenty years following her death, Chinese women in remote villages would ask, "When will the Heavenly Book visitor come again?" Their testimony about her was, "How she loved us."[40]

One year following Lottie's death, Agnes Osborne suggested the annual Women's Missionary Union foreign missions offering be taken as a living memorial to Lottie Moon, noting that Lottie's suggestions launched the offering to begin with. In 1918 Annie Armstrong, for whom Southern Baptists' home missions offering was established, said, "Miss Moon is the one who suggested the Christmas offering for foreign missions. She showed us the way in so many things. Wouldn't it be appropriate to name the offering in her memory?"[41] The issue was settled, and the rest is history.

Following her death fellow missionaries came in possession of her Bible. On the flyleaf words were found which she had penned that remain to this day a perpetual encouragement to those who go for Christ to the nations, "O, that I could consecrate myself, soul and body, to his service forever; O, that I could give myself up to him, so as never more to attempt to be my own or to have any will or affection improper for those conformed to him."[42] She did. Will you?

CHAPTER 5

Let All the Nations Give God Glory: A Passion in the Life and Martyrdom of Jim Elliot[1]

Psalm 96

 A true and genuine movement of our great God will cause the church to look *up* to heaven, catching a vision of his greatness; *in* to view our own desperate sinfulness apart from his grace; and *out* to see the lostness of the nations cut off from his goodness.

Such a movement of God engulfed and baptized the man and missionary Jim Elliot who would passionately seek to extend the glory of God among the nations. He would do this only to see his earthly life, and those of his four faithful companions, end at the age of twenty-nine in martyrdom among the Auca Indians in Ecuador. Elliot's was the same life span God granted to another missionary by the name of David Brainerd (1718–1747).

Neither Jim's life, or indeed any of these lives, was a loss. On the contrary, more of the nations were added to give God glory because of their radical devotion to "the LORD [who] is great and greatly to be praised" (v. 4 NKJV).

I think James Boice captures the full impact of Psalm 96 when he says, "It is a joyful hymn to the God of Israel as king and an invitation to the nations of the world to join Israel in praising Him. It is also a prophecy of a future day when God will judge the entire world in righteousness."[2]

It is this type of theology that drove Jim Elliot to give his life as a missionary and that inspired him to pray, "Oh that God would make us dangerous."[3] It is this kind of theology that will not let you be satisfied with a shallow, impotent, useless and comfortable Christianity. It requires more! It inspires more!

This psalm has four major movements that focus on the desires of God in relation to the nations. What does he want? What does he rightly deserve?

God Desires that the Nations Praise Him (Ps. 96:1–3)

God is identified as the Lord (Yahweh) eleven times in this psalm. Here all the earth (v. 11) is invited to praise him. Three aspects of praise are specified.

We Should Sing a New Song (Ps. 96:1)

Three times we are called to "sing to the Lord" in verses 1–2. Here it is said we should sing "a new song." The new song is the good news of his salvation "from day to day" (v. 2). It looks back to his mighty acts of deliverance, especially the exodus, but it also looks forward to the greatest act of salvation in Jesus Christ, witnessed climatically in Revelation 5:9–10 and 14:3–5:

And they sang a new song, saying; "You are worthy to take the scroll, and to open its seals; for You were slain, and have redeemed us to God by Your blood out of every tribe and tongue and people and nation, and have made us kings and priests to our God; and we shall reign on the earth. (Rev. 5:9–10 NKJV).

They sang as it were a new song before the throne, before the four living creatures, and the elders; and no one could learn that song except the hundred and forty-four thousand who were redeemed from the earth. These are the ones who were not defiled with women, for they are virgins. These are the ones who follow the Lamb wherever He goes. These were redeemed from among men, being firstfruits to God and to the Lamb. And in their mouth was found no deceit, for they are without fault before the throne of God. (Rev. 14:3–5 NKJV)

The new song of salvation will be sung by all the nations!

We Should Proclaim His Salvation (Ps. 96:2)

The three imperatives "sing" are paralleled by three additional imperatives in verses 2–3: "bless, proclaim, declare." Singing to the Lord we bless his name, we honor and give glory to the name of the Lord (Yahweh). We do this as we "proclaim the good news of his salvation from day to day" (NKJV). The idea is that not a day goes by, not a moment passes, that our hearts and minds and mouths are not occupied with the wonder of his salvation (v. 3).

We Should Declare His Glory (Ps. 96:3)

The new song (v. 1) and good news (v. 2) of the Lord's salvation demands a universal, worldwide declaration. The glory of this God must be declared among the nations and His wonders among all peoples.

Eugene Peterson paraphrases it this way in *The Message*, "Shout the news of his victory from sea to sea, take the news of his glory to the lost, news of His wonders to one and all!"

This was the passion of Philip James Elliot. Born in 1926 in Portland, Oregon, God blessed him with a father who was an itinerant evangelist. While he was not an educated man, Fred Elliot's love and devotion to Christ would significantly shape the life of his son. Of his father he would write in a letter to his future wife Elisabeth, whom he called Betty:

> Betty, I blush to think of things I have said, as if I knew something about what Scripture teaches. I know nothing. My father's religion is of a sort which I have seen nowhere else. His theology is wholly undeveloped, but so real and practical a thing that it shatters every "system" of doctrine I have seen. He cannot define theism, but he knows God. We've had some happy times together, and I cannot estimate what enrichment a few months' working with him might do for me, practically and spiritually.[4]

His journal adds this, dated January 29: "When I think of how far he has gone into the secret riches of the Father's purposes in Christ, I am shamed to silence. O Lord, let me learn tenderness and silence in my spirit, fruits of Thy knowledge. Burn, burden, break me."[5]

Jim's home was often visited by missionaries, and at about the age of eight, he trusted Jesus as his Savior. As a teen the thought of being a missionary was already in his heart. It is never too early to consider such life decisions! He was a fine athlete who saw sports as a helpful way of preparing his body for the rigors of the mission field.

He enrolled at Wheaton College in 1948, joined the wrestling team, began speaking to youth groups, started journaling in his junior year, and met Betty.

In June 1950 Jim's passion to see the nations praise the Lord Jesus saw his heart drawn to the remote and greatly feared Huaorani tribe in Ecuador, known in that day as the "Aucas." Two written pieces capture what God had placed in his heart. The first is a letter to his parents dated August 8, 1950:

> Surely those who know the great passionate heart of Jehovah must deny their own loves to share in the statement of His. Consider the call from the Throne above, Go ye, and from round about, Come over and help us, and even the call from the damned souls below, send Lazarus to my brothers, that they come not to this place. Impelled, then, by these voices, I dare not stay home while Quichuas perish. So what if the well-fed church in the homeland needs stirring? They have the Scriptures, Moses, and the Prophets, and a whole lot more. Their condemnation is written on their bank books and in the dust on their Bible covers. American believers have sold their lives to the service of Mammon, and God has His rightful way of dealing with those who succumb to the spirit of Laodicea.[6]

The second is a journal entry dated July 26, 1952: "Oh for a faith that sings! . . . Lord God, give me a faith that will take sufficient quiver out of me so that I may sing! Over the Aucas, Father I want to sing."[7]

God Desires That the Nations Fear Him (Ps. 96:4–6)

A right theology of God will lead to a healthy reverence, even fear and awe of Him. He will not be insulted as "the man upstairs" or "my buddy and pal." "J. C. is my homeboy" will be dismissed for the dishonoring and disrespectful sham that it is. No, this God is the omnipotent, omniscient, omnipresent Sovereign of the universe who is coming "to judge the earth . . . the world with righteousness" (v. 13 NKJV).

The psalmist, therefore, says fear him! Why? Two reasons are given.

First, we should fear him because he is a great God. Our God is a great God and greatly (v. 4 NIV, "most worthy") to be praised. He is to be feared above all the other gods. Why? Because the gods of the peoples are idols, false gods, imposters, no gods at all. They are scattered around the globe enslaving millions to false idols and false systems of religion that are an expressway to hell. The Lord is great and they are not. He saves and they damn. The Lord is really something and they are really nothing. The Lord made everything. They have made nothing.

Second, we should fear him because he is a glorious God. Four marvelous affirmations are made of the great redeemer and Creator God in verse 6. These are truths the nations need to know. Honor (NASB, "splendor") is before him, radiating from his person. Majesty is before him, flooding forth from him. Strength is found in his sanctuary, his royal residence. Beauty is found in his sanctuary, his kingly court. Standing before the great God like "throne room attendants," honor, majesty, strength, and beauty bear witness to the God who is awesome and like no other.

Elisabeth Elliot said of her husband, "Jim's aim was to know God."[8] Jim himself would write, "Lord, make my way prosperous, not that I achieve high station, but that my life may be an exhibit to the value of knowing God."[9] Jim Elliot saw our God for who he is and a holy reverence and fear attended him while at Wheaton and drove him to take the gospel to the Aucas.

Note these journal entries:[10]

July 15, 1948

How like Orpah I am—prone to kiss, to display full devotion and turn away; how unlike Ruth, cleaving and refusing to part except at death (1:14–17). Eternal Lover, make Thou Thyself inseparable from my unstable soul. Be Thou the object bright and fair to fill and satisfy the heart. My hope to meet Thee in the air, and nevermore from Thee to part![11]

October 27, 1948

Sense a great need of my Father tonight. Have feelings of what Dr. Jaarsma [philosophy professor at Wheaton] calls "autonomous man" in another context. I do not feel needy enough. Sufficiency in myself is a persistent thought, though I try to judge it. Lord Jesus, Tender Lover of this brute soul, wilt Thou make me weak? I long to understand Thy sufficiency and my inadequacy, and how can I sense this except in experience? So, Lord, Thou knowest what I am able to bear. Send trouble that I might know peace; send anxiety that I might know rest in Thee. Send hard things that I may learn to rely on Thy dissolving them. Strange askings, and I do not know what I speak, but "my desire is toward Thee"—anything that will intensify and make me tender, Savior. I desire to be like Thee, Thou knowest.[12]

October 28, 1948

Wonderful season of intercession . . . tonight. "At thy right hand are pleasures . . ." (Ps. 16:11). Prayed a strange prayer today. I covenanted with my Father that He would do either of two things—either glorify Himself to the utmost in me, or slay me. By His grace I shall not have His second best. For He heard me, I believe, so that now I have nothing to look forward to but a life of sacrificial sonship (that's how thy Savior was glorified, my soul) or heaven soon. Perhaps tomorrow. What a prospect![13]

November 1, 1948

Son of Man, I feel it would be best if I should be taken now to Thy throne. I dread causing Thee shame at Thy appearing (Mark 8:38). Father, take my life, yea, my blood if Thou wilt, and consume it with Thine enveloping fire. I would not save it, for it is not mine to save. Have it, Lord, have it all. Pour out my life as an oblation for the world. Blood is only of value as it flows before Thine altar.[14]

Here we find the words, the heart, of a man who rightly feared the Lord. How strange his words sound to the convenient Christianity that has engulfed our churches. We would say he is a fanatic. What would Jesus say? What he had we desperately need. What he had must be shared.

God Desires That the Nations Worship Him (*Ps. 96:7–9*)

Warren Wiersbe says, "Praise means looking up, but worship means bowing down."[15] It means to acknowledge and ascribe to God his worth and value by humbling ourselves before him and submitting to his will for our lives.

Three times in this third stanza we are commanded to "give" or "ascribe" glory to God, a glory that rightly belongs only to Him and a glory that should come from the "families of the nations" (NIV). These words are almost identical to the beginning of Psalm 29. There the angels are called to worship the Lord. Here it is the nations. What are we to give to the great and greatly to be praised God?

First, we are to give him honor, according to verses 7–8. All the nations are summoned to give the Lord acknowledgement of his glory and strength, glory due to the name of Yahweh, the name above all names that Philippians 2:9–11 informs us, is the name of Jesus. The honor he rightly deserves is proven by an offering that is brought into his presence. The apostle Paul will speak of our giving our bodies as an offering, as "living sacrifices" to King Jesus (Rom. 12:1).

Second, we are to acknowledge his holiness according to verse 9. We honor Him because of the beauty or splendor of his holiness, his moral perfection, his utter transcendence and greatness. In light of our sinfulness and depravity, our finitude and creaturliness, we and all the earth rightly tremble before such a God. No doing "the wave" before this God. No "three cheers for Jesus" from those who see him for who he is and see us for who we are without him.

Again, I believe there is much to learn from the life and martyrdom of Jim Elliot, in his own words from his journal.

November 6, 1948

Forgive me for being so ordinary while claiming to know so extraordinary a God.[16]

September 19, 1948

To worship in truth is not sufficient, that is to worship in true form. There must be exercise of the spirit; the new man must be stirred to action; we must have spiritual worship. Philippians 3:3: We have mention of emotional worship—rejoicing in soul as well as exercising in spirit. Paul has spoken of rejoicing in the Gospel's furtherance (1:18); in the sending of Epaphroditus (2:25), and now he says, "Finally, rejoice in the Lord" (3:1). Not in fellowship or in privileges, but in the Lord. "Delight thyself also in the Lord" (Ps. 37:4). Then Romans 12:1, 2 gives us rational worship, involving the presentation of our bodies. Yea, Lord, make me a true worshiper![17]

September 20, 1948

2 Chronicles 20. I cannot explain the yearnings of my heart this morning. Cannot bring myself to study or to pray for any length of time. Oh, what a jumble of cross-currented passions I am—a heart so deceitful it deceives itself. May Christ satisfy my thirst, may the river Rock pour out Himself to me in this desert place. Nothing satisfies—not nature, or fellowship with any, but only my Eternal Lover. Ah, how cold my heart is toward Him. But "our eyes are upon Thee" (v. 12). Possibility of seeing Betty again brings back wistful

thoughts. *[Betty is Elisabeth whom he would eventually marry. They would serve together in Ecuador and have one child together, Valerie].* How I hate myself for such weakness! Is not Christ enough, Jim? What need you more—a woman—in His place? Nay, God forbid. I shall have Thee, Lord Jesus. Thou didst buy me, now I must buy Thee. Thou knowest how reluctant I am to pay, because I do not value Thee sufficiently. I am Thine at terrible cost to Thyself. Now Thou must become mine—as Thou didst not attend to the price, neither would I.[18]

August 16, 1954

Because O God, from Thee comes all, because from Thine own mouth has entered us the power to breathe, from Thee the sea of air in which we swim and the unknown nothingness that stays it over us with unseen bonds; because Thou gavest us from heart of love so tender, mind so wise and hand so strong, Salvation; because Thou are Beginning, God, I worship Thee.

Because Thou are the end of every way, the goal of man; because to Thee shall come of every people respect and praise; their emissaries find Thy throne their destiny; because Ethiopia shall stretch out her hands to Thee, babes sing Thy praise; because Thine altar gives to sparrows shelter, sinners peace, and devils fury; because "to Thee shall all flesh come"; because Thou art Omega. Praise.

Because Thou sure art set to justify that Son of Thine and wilt in time make known just who He is and soon will send Him back to show Himself; because the Name of Jesus has been laughingly nailed upon a cross and is just now on earth held very lightly and Thou wilt bring that Name to light; because, O God of righteousness, Thou wilt do right by my Lord, Jesus Christ, I worship Thee.[19]

God Desires That the Nations Enjoy Him (Ps. 96:10–13)

John Piper loves to say, "God is most glorified in us when we are most satisfied in Him."[20] In other words God wants us, he wants the nations, to enjoy him. We could spend all of eternity listing the reasons we should enjoy our great God, but Psalm 96 highlights two reasons that shine like the sun announcing the glory and goodness of God.

First, we enjoy him because he is a sovereign King according to verses 10–12. The nations must hear that this God reigns, he rules sovereignly over the whole earth. He made it ("the world is firmly established") and he maintains it ("it shall not be moved"). He's got the whole world in his hands.

He shall judge the peoples righteously. No one will ever point a finger at God and say, "You were not fair. You did me wrong." You cannot bribe this God. He plays no favorites in judging the nations. Here is one judge you can always count on to do the right thing.

In light of all this enjoy him!
Let the heavens rejoice.
Let the earth be glad.
Let the sea roar and all that is in it.
Let the field be joyful and all that is in it.

In antiphonal response "all the trees of the forest will rejoice before Yahweh, before the LORD."

Second, we enjoy him because he is a righteous King according to verse 13. This psalm ends on an eschatological note, a note of hope for those who love and enjoy him, a note of warning for those who reject his rightful lordship over their lives. He is coming to judge the earth. He is coming to judge the world with righteousness. He is coming to judge the peoples with His truth. What does this look like? Revelation 19:11–16 has the answer:

> Now I saw heaven opened, and behold, a white horse. And He who sat on him was called Faithful and True, and in righteousness He judges and makes war. His eyes were like a flame of fire, and on His head were many crowns. He had a name written that no one knew except Himself. He was clothed with a robe dipped in blood, and His name is called The Word of God. And the armies in heaven, clothed in fine linen, white and clean, followed Him on white horses. Now out of His mouth goes a sharp sword, that with it He should strike the nations. And He Himself will rule them with a rod of iron. He Himself treads the winepress of the fierceness and wrath of Almighty God. And He has on His robe and on His thigh a name written: KING OF KINGS AND LORD OF LORDS. (NKJV)

Conclusion

Jim Elliot wrote in a letter to his family: "Remember you are immortal until your work is done. But don't let the sands of time get into the eyes of your vision to reach those who still sit in darkness. They simply must hear."[21] Just before he left for the last time, Elisabeth asked Jim if they were attacked by the Aucas, would they use their guns? Jim's response was clear and certain: "We will not use our guns!" When Elisabeth asked why, he simply said, "Because we are ready for heaven, but they are not."[22]

On January 8, 1956, Jim Elliot, along with Ed McCully, Roger Youderian, Pete Fleming, and Nate Saint, waited hopefully for another meeting with the Auca or Huaorani Indians, having had several friendly encounters in previous days. However, a group of ten Huaorani men attacked the five missionaries and brutally murdered them. Jim Elliot's mutilated body was found downstream in the river. There was no funeral, no tombstone for a memorial. However, on resurrection day the glorified bodies of these champions for Jesus will rise from the dirt of Ecuador! Jim left behind his wife Elizabeth and a baby girl. They had been married less than three years.

On January 30, 1956, *Life Magazine* published a ten-page article on the martyrdom of these men entitled, "'Go ye and preach the Gospel'—five devout Americans in remote Ecuador follow this precept and are killed."[23]

Our nation was shocked, and Christians all over the world wept. Jim would have been embarrassed by this. In a letter to his parents dated June 23, 1947, he wrote, "Missionaries are very human folks, just doing what they are asked. Simply a bunch of nobodies trying to exalt Somebody."[24]

And in a letter to his mother dated August 16, 1948, Jim wrote, "Oh what a privilege to be made a minister of the things of the 'happy God.' I only hope that He will let me preach to those who have never heard that name Jesus. What else is worthwhile in this life? I have heard nothing better. 'Lord, send me!'"[25]

In his final note to his wife Elizabeth, dated January 4 and found on the river beach where he died, Elliot wrote, "Our hopes are up but no sign of the 'neighbors' yet. Perhaps today is the day the Aucas will be reached. . . . We're going down now, pistols, gifts, novelties in our pockets, prayer in our hearts. All for now. Your lover, Jim."[26]

Jim Elliot's journal entry of October 28, 1949, is famous.
Do not miss its context, or you will miss a marvelous blessing.
I will allow Jim's journal to speak for itself. No commentary
will be needed.

October 27

Enjoyed much sweetness in the reading of the last
months of Brainerd's life. How consonant are his
thoughts to my own regarding the "true and false religion of this late day." Saw, in reading him, the value
of these notations and was much encouraged to think
of a life of godliness in the light of an early death. . . .
I have prayed for new men, fiery, reckless men, possessed of uncontrollably youthful passion—these lit
by the Spirit of God. I have prayed for new words,
explosive, direct, simple words. I have prayed for new
miracles. Explaining old miracles will not do. If God is
to be known as the God who does wonders in heaven
and earth, then God must produce for this generation.
Lord, fill preachers and preaching with Thy power.
How long dare we go on without tears, without moral
passions, hatred and love? Not long, I pray, Lord Jesus,
not long.[27]

October 28

One of the great blessings of heaven is the appreciation of heaven on earth—Ephesian truth. He is no fool
who gives what he cannot keep to gain that which he
cannot lose.[28]

Jim Elliot said, "Our orders are: the gospel to every creature."[29] Because he believed this he also said:

Nothing is too good to be: so believe, believe to see. In my own experience I have found that the most extravagant dreams of boyhood have not surpassed the great experience of being in the will of God, and I believe that nothing could be better. That is not to say that I do not want other things, and other ways of living, and other places to see, but in my right mind I know that my hopes and plans for myself could not be any better than He has arranged and fulfilled them. Thus may we all find it, and know the truth of the Word which says, 'He will be our guide even until death.'"[30]

Jim did give up that which he could not keep to gain that which he could not lose. Now the question is before us: Will I? Will you? Oh God, give us more Jim Elliots that all the nations may give you glory!

CHAPTER 6

The Cross and Faithful Ministry As Seen in the Pastoral and Missionary Ministry of George Leile: First Baptist Missionary to the Nations

Galatians 6:11–18

 He was the first Baptist to leave his homeland and take the gospel to foreign soil. Immediately many of you will think that I speak of William Carey who is rightly called "the father of the modern missionary movement," who left England in 1793 taking the gospel to India. But you would be wrong in your assessment. So, you might think I had in mind Adoniram Judson, "the father of the American Baptist missionary movement," who in 1812 left America to take the gospel to the hostile land of Burma where he, like Carey, would labor for King Jesus for forty years. Once again you would draw an inaccurate conclusion.

The man I believe is the pioneer of Baptists missions was a black man and a former slave by the name of George Leile, who, as one biographer noted, "was led by the living hand of a smiling Providence,"[1] to plant the gospel in Jamaica in 1782. Thus he predates Carey as a missionary to the nations by more than a decade! Here is a modern missions grandfather. Leroy Fitts says it well, "The black Baptist church was born a missionary movement."[2]

In the man George Leile we find the heartbeat for ministry and missions joined to that of the apostle Paul, who wrote in Galatians 6:14, "But far be it from me to boast except in the cross of our Lord Jesus Christ, by which the world had been crucified to me, and I to the world" (ESV). Here we find the grounding for faithful ministry and a passion for missions. Here we find in verses 11–18 a pattern for a cross-centered ministry, for a life for those who are willing to "bear in their own body the marks, the brands, the *stigmata* of the Lord Jesus" (6:17). Four marks of such a man stand out.

A Cross-Centered Ministry Is Humble Not Prideful
(*Gal. 6:11–13*)

Paul has spent six chapters expounding the gracious nature of salvation apart from human effort. So concerned was he about any compromise of this message that he begins and ends the letter on a note of "grace" (1:3; 6:18). Further, he penned at least the end of the epistle, if not the whole letter, with his "own hand" in "large letters" (6:11), which may give evidence of an eye affliction he may have received from the Lord when converted on the Damascus Road (Acts 9:9; cf. 2 Cor 12:7–10).

In Galatians 6:12–13 (NKJV), Paul rips into those who through pride "desire to make a good showing in the flesh" and impress others by what they do. He notes they are motivated by a self-interested agenda: "that they may not suffer persecu-tion for the cross of Christ" (v. 12 NKJV). Further, they are hypocrites! They do not keep the Mosaic Law themselves but do boast about the numbers they can tally up in terms of those they win to their team! John MacArthur sums up well the disposition of these false teachers and unconverted ministers, "They did everything possible to call attention to themselves, glorying in the recognition and praise they received because of their positions, titles and converts."[3]

Edmund Clowney tells the story, "On one occasion I had tea with Martyn Lloyd-Jones in Ealing, London, and decided to ask him a question that concerned me. "'Dr. Lloyd-Jones,' I said, 'How can I tell whether I am preaching in the energy of the flesh or in the power of the Spirit?' 'That is very easy,' Lloyd-Jones replied, as I shriveled. 'If you are preaching in the energy of the flesh, you will feel exalted and lifted up. If you are preaching in the power of the Spirit, you will feel awe and humility.'"[4]

How contrary the mind-set of pride and boasting is to a cross-centered minister; boasting in what I can do and manipulating others for further self-glorying! How contrary this mind-set is to what we see in the life and ministry of Jesus, Paul, and a man named George Leile. Edward Holmes Jr. called him "one of the unsung heroes of religious history."[5]

He was born a slave on a plantation in Virginia around 1750. These are humble beginnings to be sure, but it was not the fact that he came into this world a slave of men that fostered his humility but the fact he gladly saw himself as a slave of Jesus Christ. Through the influence of a godly father and the faithful preaching of a Baptist pastor named Matthew Moore, George Leile was born into the kingdom and called to a ministry that would take him to the nations. In his own hand he wrote in 1791 from Kingston, Jamaica:

I was born in Virginia, my father's name was Liele[6] [*sic*], and my mother's name Nancy; I cannot ascertain much of them, as I went to several parts of America when young, and at length resided in new Georgia; but was informed both by white and black people, that *my father was the only black person who knew the Lord in a spiritual way in that country.* I always had a natural fear of God from my youth, and was often checked in conscience with thoughts of death, which barred me from many sins and bad company. I knew no other way at that time to hope for salvation but only in the performance of my good works.[7]

In 1773, at the age of twenty-three, Leile was converted to Christ. Speaking of that experience that came after six months distress of mind and inquiring the way of life (or what we call "seeking the Lord"), Leile said:

I saw my condemnation in my own heart, and I found no way wherein I could escape the damnation of hell, only through the merits of my dying Lord and Savior Jesus Christ; which caused me to make intercession with Christ, for the salvation of my poor immortal soul; and I full well recollect, I requested of my Lord and Master to give me a work, I did not care how mean it was, only to try and see how good I would do it.[8]

Matthew Moore, a white minister, would baptize Leile. Following Leile's dramatic conversion, his owner, a kind and godly Baptist deacon named Henry Sharp, gave him his free-dom that he might exercise his gifts and fulfill his calling that had been given to him by the Lord. A genuine humility would mark this man of God throughout the ministry and mission given to him by our Savior. Leile was ordained on May 20,

1775, and is recognized as the first ordained black Baptist pastor in Georgia. In Savannah, Georgia, he would found the first "African Baptist Church in North America, a church still in existence today."[9]

One will look in vain for any pride or boastfulness for these or any other of his many accomplishments. Bi-vocational all his life, Leile would, without complaint, support himself, his wife and four children by whatever jobs he could find. In a letter to Dr. Rippon of London, he shared:

> I cannot tell what is my age, as I have no account of the time of my birth. . . . I have a wife and four children. My wife [her name was Hannah] was baptized by me in Savannah, and *I have every satisfaction in life from her.* She is much the same age as myself. [My four children], *are all members of the church.* My occupation is a farmer, but as the seasons of this part of the country are uncertain, I also keep a team of horses and wagons for the carrying of goods from one place to another, which I attend myself, with the assistance of my sons, and by this way of life have gained the good will of the public, who recommended me to the business and to some very principal work for the government.[10]

As a cross-centered minister, he was humble not prideful. He gratefully accepted the sovereign assignment given to him by his Lord.

A Cross-Centered Ministry Glories in Christ Not Ourselves (*Gal. 6:14–15*)

Charles Spurgeon said Galatians 6:14 "was the theme of [Paul's] ministry."[11] In contrast to false teachers who boast and brag about their accomplishments, who they are, who they

know, where they serve, what they have done, Paul declares in
the strongest possible language "But God forbid" (NKJV). The
text literally reads, "But to me not it will be." No, I will not
boast in me in any way. But I will boast in *someone* and *something* else. I will boast in the cross of our Lord Jesus Christ.
Others were ashamed of the cross, embarrassed by the cross.
Others viewed it as foolishness and nonsense. A poor Galilean
Jew hanging on a first-century gallow is not something you
boast in. It is something you recoil from, run from, turn away
from. Not for me, says Paul. I will only boast in "the cross of
our Lord Jesus Christ."

George Whitefield rightly states, "Do not talk of God
being your glory, if you do not love his cross."[12] But why
must this be? The cross is the ground of my assurance that
I have been made new in Christ and accepted by God (vv.
14–15). The cross is the place where the wrath of God was
poured out on another that it might not be poured out on
me. It is on the cross I am united to Christ; I died to this
world and all its claims on my life. The cross is the place
where all self-glorying was put to death that I might glory
and delight only in Jesus. The cross of Christ is the message
I proclaim, the ministry I perform, the miracle that made
me a new person.

Listen to how Charles Spurgeon so wonderfully captures
the heart of what Paul is after in his sermon entitled "Grand
Glorying":

> The Apostle adds, "By which the world is crucified
> unto me, and I unto the world." There are two crosses
> in that saying—there is the world crucified, there, and
> there is Paul crucified, here. What means he by this?
> Why, he means that ever since he fell in love with
> Jesus Christ, he lost all love for the world! It seemed

to him to be a poor, crucified, dying thing, and he turned away from it just as you would from a criminal whom you might see hanging in chains—and would desire to go anywhere rather than see the poor being. So Paul seemed to see the world on gallows—hung up there. "There," he said, "that is what I think of you and all your pomp, and all your power, and all your wealth, and all your fame! You are on the gallows, a malefactor, nailed up, crucified! I would not give a fig for you! I would not turn on my heels to speak to you—all that you could give me would no more suit my taste than as if husks were given to me. Give them to your own swine and let them fatten thereon!" . . . And now observe the other Cross. There is Paul on that. The world thinks as little of Paul as Paul does of the world. The world says, "Oh, the harebrained Paul! He was once sensible, but he has gone mad upon that stubborn notion about the Crucified one! The man is a fool." So the world crucifies him. . . . So is it with the world and the genuine Christian. If he glories in Christ, he must expect to be misunderstood, misrepresented and attacked. And, on the other hand, he will say that he would sooner have the world's scorn than its honor! He would sooner have its hate than its love, for the love of the world is enmity against God. Blessed are you when they shall say all manner of evil against you falsely for Christ's sake and the Gospel's. Set your account, you Christians, upon rough weather and get seaworthy vessels that will stand a gale or two! Ask the Lord to give you Grace enough to suffer and endure for that precious Savior who will give you reward enough when you see Him face to face, for one hour with Him will make up for it all! Therefore, be faithful, and may the Lord help you thus to glory in the Cross of Christ. Amen.[13]

With the man George Leile, it was the same.

After his conversion Leile preached for two years in the slave quarters of plantations surrounding Savannah, even making his way into South Carolina. Many black slaves came to Christ as a result of his powerful preaching. As noted earlier, it was about this time that Leile's master, Henry Sharp, freed him. Sharp, however, was killed in the Revolutionary War in 1778, and Sharp's heirs sought to reenslave Leile. They had Leile thrown in jail, but he was able to produce his "free papers."[14] Then borrowing $700 for passage for himself and his family, he left Savannah as an indentured servant and in 1782 landed in Kingston, Jamaica.[15] What men had meant for evil God had meant for good! The hand of providential sovereignty selected him to take the gospel to Jamaica as the first Baptist missionary in history. He would be faithful in this ministry assignment.

Eventually Leile paid off his debt and was free once more. This cross-centered man set about the business of preaching Christ to a people in need of both spiritual and personal emancipation. Holmes says it so well, "Now free himself, he was filled with compassion by the wretched condition of the slaves in Jamaica."[16]

He immediately formed a church with four others (one being his wife) from America, and he would begin public preaching services at the Kingston Race Course! He shared in a letter that "preaching took very good effect with the poorer sort, especially the slaves. The people at first persecuted us, both at meetings and baptisms, but God be praised, they seldom interrupt us now."[17] During eight years of preaching, Leile baptized five hundred persons and established a strong church in Kingston. Again giving evidence of his humility and desire to glory only in Christ, he sent urgent appeals to the British Baptist to send missionaries. As a wise minister, he gladly shared the growing work with other capable co-laborers.

As a result of his gospel ministry, slaves in Jamaica would be emancipated on July 31, 1833. This road to freedom was not easy, and Leile himself would suffer for his Master, King Jesus, and those whom he loved and cared for. Sometime prior to 1802, "Mr. Leile was charged with preaching sedition, for which he was thrown into prison, loaded with irons, and his feet fastened in stocks. Not even his wife or children were permitted to see him. At length he was tried for his life; but no evil could be proved against him, and he was honorably acquitted."[18]

This freedom was short-lived when Leile was thrown in jail again. This time "for a balance due to the builder of his chapel. He refused to take the benefit of the insolvent Debtor's Act, and remained in prison until he had fully paid all that was due."[19] Much of the expense of the chapel and others costs had come from Leile's contributions, and he also "labored without fee or reward, supporting himself by the work of his own hands."[20]

"In 1805 the Assembly enacted a law forbidding all preaching to the slaves. Though the law was not always vigorously enforced uniformly until 1810, there were numerous instances of the severest persecution in the forms of whipping and brutal murder. Numerous instances of brutality, sexual abuse, imprisonment, lashings, and murder were reported by numbers of observers and missionaries during the years between 1802 and 1834, when slavery was abolished throughout the British Commonwealth. However, it was July 31, 1838, before all vestiges of slavery were eradicated from Jamaica."[21]

Only a man devoted to glorying in Christ crucified and not himself could endure such opposition and shameful conduct from fellow human beings. And the result of his humble perseverance: In 1814 there were only eight thousand Baptists in Jamaica, including slaves, freed men, and some whites. Only eighteen years later in 1832, there were twenty thousand Baptists in Jamaica. The genesis of this great harvest: George Leile!

Numerous converts of his were called to preach with several establishing churches in Savannah, Georgia; Nova Scotia, and Sierra Leone. The man was not only one who was sent; he was also a sender as well! Clarence Wagner gets it right when he states:

> George Leile, a black slave, is the first recorded licensed and ordained Black Baptist Preacher-Missionary in America. The initiator of foreign missions among Black Baptist in the world. Our black Baptist heritage stems from the seeds planted by him in the soils of difficulty in America, Jamaica and Africa. Those seeds were incubated by the love of Jesus Christ, germinated by the power of the Holy Spirit and protected by the infallibility of God's Holy Word.[22]

A Cross-Centered Ministry Walks in Truth Not Error (*Gal. 6:16*)

The call to ministry is inherently theological. As preachers of the gospel and teachers of the Word, it could never be any other way. The idea of a nontheological minister is nonsense. It is complete and utter foolishness. This is why Paul places the cross and all it entails at the center of the Christian life and ministry (v. 14). It is why he stresses so strongly the doctrine of a new creation made possible by union of Christ (v. 15 NKJV). It is why he now challenges the Galatians and us in verse 16 to "walk according to this rule" where peace and mercy may be found upon Gentile and Jew alike. Timothy George puts it like this, "[Paul] invokes the peace and mercy of God upon those . . . who remain faithful to the truth of the gospel Paul had originally preached among them."[23]

Once more this reminds us that theology matters, that theology is important, that good, sound gospel-centered theology is essential to both the health and life of the church. Ultimately this is something for which the whole church is responsible. Initially, it is something for which ministries will be held accountable (cf. Heb 13:7, 17). In applying these truths to those who minister the word and who are called to protect the flock from the vultures of theological error, Don Carson says, "The cross stands as the test and the standard of all vital Christian ministry. The cross not only establishes what we are to preach, but how we are to preach. It prescribes what Christian leaders must be and how Christians must view Christian leaders."[24]

Great harm comes to the church if we separate ministry from theology, preaching from doctrine, and Christian care from conviction. In far too many cases today, the pastor's ministry has been evacuated of serious doctrinal content, and many pastors seem to have little connection to or even concern for any sense of theological vocation. All this must be reversed if the church is to remain true to God's Word and the gospel. Unless the pastor functions as a pastor/theologian and missionary/evangelist, the church is left with no leader or example at the top of what it means to live the cross-centered life.

George Leile received no formal education as far as we know. However, to consider him illiterate, uneducated, or theologically ill prepared would be an erroneous judgment of

unforgivable proportion. The great scholar of the history of
preaching, Hughes Oliphant Old, says of Leile, "His preaching
was received by black and white alike. . . . George Leile was
a gifted evangelistic preacher who knew how to present the
gospel in the language of his people."[25] Some even compared
his style to that of George Whitefield.

In a letter to Dr. Rippon of London dated 1891, Leile
wrote, "I have a few books, some good old authors and ser-
mons, and one large Bible that was given me by a gentleman.
. . . I agree to election, redemption, the Fall of Adam, regen-
eration and perseverance, knowing the promise is to all who
endure, in grace, faith and good works to the end, shall be
saved."[26] In appealing to the Honorable House of Assembly
in Jamaica for freedom to worship, he said they only "desired
liberty to worship Almighty God, according to the tenets of
the Bible."[27]

The black missionary minister and church planter was a
Calvinist in the same vein as Brainerd, Carey, Judson, Rice,
and Moon. He saw no dichotomy between the sacred assignment of pastor/theologian and missionary/evangelist. What a
model for ministry he provides. And, the result of the ministry of a man who walked so faithfully in the truth? Hear
the words of one of his converts, called himself to the gospel
ministry under Leile:

> I am one of the poor, unworthy, helpless creatures,
> born in this island, whom our glorious Master, Jesus
> Christ, was graciously pleased to call from a state of
> darkness to the marvelous light of the gospel; and
> since our Lord hath bestowed his mercy on my soul,
> our beloved minister [Leile], by the consent of the
> church appointed me deacon, school-master, and his
> principal helper. We have great reason in this island

to praise and glorify the Lord, for his goodness and loving-kindness, in sending his blessed gospel amongst us, by our well-beloved minister, brother Leile. We were living in slavery to sin and Satan, and the Lord hath redeemed our souls to a state of happiness, to praise his glorious and ever-blessed name; and we hope to enjoy everlasting peace by the promise of our Lord and Master, Jesus Christ. The blessed gospel is spreading wonderfully in this island: believers are daily coming into the church; and we hope in a little time to see Jamaica become a Christian country. I remain, respectfully, Rev. and dear Sir, your poor brother in Christ, Thomas Nicholas Swigle.[28]

A Cross-Centered Ministry Seeks to Please God Not Man (*Gal. 6:17–18*)

C. J. Mahaney says, "Too many of us have stopped concentrating on the wonders of Jesus crucified."[29] Then, so as to apply this truth deeply and personally to our souls, he writes, "On a daily basis we're faced with two simple choices. We can either *listen* to ourselves and our constantly changing feelings about our circumstances, or we can *talk* to ourselves about the unchanging truth of who God is and what He's accomplished for us at the cross through His Son Jesus."[30]

The apostle Paul clearly opted for the latter as should we. In essence he says, "I will not allow myself any longer to be troubled, harassed, or bothered by the agendas of men, demons, circumstances, or feelings. Why? Because I am a marked man! I bear in my body the branding, the *stigmata* of the Lord Jesus! His cross is my cross. He has marked me as his slave and 'his insignia is in my very flesh.'"[31] His words reflect his earlier declaration in Galatians 1:10! I am a Christ pleaser

not a man pleaser. He died for me! He bought me! He loves
me! He called me! His grace is with me! (v. 18).

A marked man will serve the church of the Lord Jesus and
seek the souls of the lost with a particular perspective and passion. Jonathan Edwards put it like this:

> The thing that Christ did in shedding [his blood
> for the salvation and happiness of souls] should be
> regarded by ministers as their example and direc-
> tion. If Christ so loved the souls of men as to lay out
> Himself and deny Himself at this rate for the salvation
> [and happiness of souls], then surely the ministers of
> Christ should be ready greatly to exert themselves and
> deny themselves and suffer for the sake of [the salva-
> tion and happiness of souls]. For as Christ often said,
> "The servant is not above his master, nor the disciple
> above his lord' [Matthew 10:24].[32]

Literally and spiritually bearing the marks of the Lord
Jesus as a joyful recipient of His grace within his spirit, George
Leile refused to be troubled when persecuted and opposed.
For example:

> On one occasion, when the church was about to
> celebrate the Lord's Supper, a gentleman (so called)
> rode into the chapel, and, urging his horse through
> the midst of the people to the very front of the pul-
> pit, exclaimed in terms of insolence and profanity,
> "Come, old Leile, give my horse the Sacrament!" Mr.
> Leile coolly replied, "No, Sir, you are not fit yourself
> to receive it." After maintaining his position for some
> time the intruder rode out.[33]

A contemporary, Stephen Cooke said of Leile's missionary ministry among the Jamaicans:

> He has been for a considerable time past, very zeal-
> ous in the ministry; but his congregation being chiefly
> slaves, they had it not in their power to support him;
> therefore, he has been obligated to do it from his own
> industry; this has taken a considerable part of his time,
> and much of his attention from his labours in the min-
> istry; however, I am led to believe that it has been of
> essential service to the cause of God, for his industry
> has set a good example to his flock, and has put it out
> of the power of enemies to religion to say, that he has
> been eating the bread of idleness or lived upon the
> poor slaves.[34]

Another, by the name of George Gibbs Bailey, said: "I have inquired of those, who, I thought, could give me an account of Mr. Leile's conduct, and I can say, with pleasure, what Pilate said, 'I can find no fault in this man.' The Baptist church thrives abundantly among the Negroes, more than any denomination in Jamaica; but I am sorry to say, the Methodist church is declining rapidly."[35]

Leile himself would say to all of this: "I have a right to praise God, and glorify him for the manifold blessings I have received, and still do receive from him. I have full liberty from Spanish-Town, the capital of this country, to teach the gospel throughout the island [Reports indicate this is exactly what he did]. The Lord is blessing the work everywhere, and believers are added daily to the church. My tongue is not able to express the goodness of the Lord."[36]

Conclusion

George Leile, like Paul, was a cross-centered man who carried out a cross-centered ministry to the nations to the end of his life. As biographer E. K. Love writes:

> When he established a church in the towns he made for the interior to unfurl the gospel banner to those who were sitting in darkness and in the region of the shadow of death. . . . We have no date of his death, nor the latter end of his life. But he will be remembered, and his name honored, both here and in Jamaica while memory holds its place. Whatever the negro Baptists here and in Jamaica are, they owe it to his humble beginning. And whatever may be written of either of us, it cannot be complete if his name is left out. His record is here, there and in heaven.[37]

Later records would indicate that Leile died in 1828. He did not see the full fruit of his labor in this life. Oh, but I suspect with the strongest certainty his Master did give him at least a glimpse of it from heaven! The summation of this cross-centered minister and missionary could not be said better than what we find in the words of Edward Holmes once more:

> Ordained in a white church in Burke County, Georgia, this freed Negro slave gathered the first Negro church in America at Silver Bluff, (Gaulphin's Mill) South Carolina. Brought up in no church by slave parents, he became the first ordained Negro Baptist minis-ter in America. Though supported by no church or denomination agency, he became the first Protestant missionary to go out from America to establish a for-eign mission, ten years before William Carey set out from England. . . . A man without formal education,

he learned to read the Bible and became a preacher of such effectiveness that in seven years in Jamaica he had converted over 500 slaves to Christianity.

Though born a Negro slave in Virginia about 1750, his illustrious service as a patriot and preacher served as a weighty influence in the abolition of slavery from his adopted land of Jamaica, in 1838. When the first English Baptist missionary reached Jamaica in 1814 there were 8,000 Baptist converts. This number grew to 20,000 Baptists in 1832, much of which growth was accomplished despite persecution by the English planters and the jailing of Leile and his followers by the government authorities.

Several of his converts became preachers who established churches in Savannah, Georgia, Nova Scotia, Sierra Leone and Jamaica. His correspondence with John Rippon, and other English Baptists, helped furnish the enthusiasm for their missionary interest and activity at home and abroad. . . .

The slave, who was himself set free to declare the glorious deliverance of his Lord, had brought the fruits of the gospel's spirit to thousands who had learned to love his Lord and accept his salvation. The Negro prophet of deliverance had raised up many courageous servants of the Lord to lead his people into their Promised Land of freedom.[38]

The Pattern of Paul's Missionary Life Revealed in the Ministry of David Brainerd for the Furtherance of the Gospel among the Nations

2 Timothy 1:8–12

 Perhaps no one has had a greater influence on the modern missionary movement than David Brainerd. John Thornbury, a biographer of Brainerd, wrote, "Only eternity will reveal how many fires of evangelistic zeal have been lit by the perusal of the account of his short but powerful life."[1] His impact on men like William Carey, Adoniram Judson, Henry Martyn, and Jim Elliott was enormous. This is all the more amazing when you consider he died at the age of twenty-nine and had a missionary ministry to the American Indians for only three years.

The power of Brainerd's influence, in large part, lies in the pattern of ministry he adopted, a pattern for service found in

the life of the apostle Paul. The parallels between the lives of
Paul and David Brainerd are striking. They are too numerous
to be merely a coincidence. Their mutual and equal commitment to the power of the gospel, the necessity of a clear and
undeniable call, a ministry of suffering, and an unsurpassing
confidence in Christ drove them as William Carey said, "to
expect great things [from God] and to attempt great things
[for God]."

The lives and ministries of these heroes of the faith, one
standing gladly in the shadow of the other, provide a model
for ministry worthy of our most careful consideration. In
2 Timothy 1:8–12 we see four characteristics of a ministry for
the furtherance of the gospel among the nations.

Unashamed of Christ and His Gospel (*2 Tim. 1:8*)

The condition in which the apostle Paul penned 2 Timothy
was that of a Roman prison. This was not his first imprisonment, but it would prove to be his last. Second Timothy was
his final letter, the benediction of his ministry. The apostle
Paul wrote with urgency, making clear that he did not expect
to avoid execution this time (2 Tim. 4:6–8). As he wrote
Timothy, his young son in the ministry, he was alone except
for the company of Doctor Luke (2 Tim. 4:11). The conditions
in the Mamertine Prison, where he possibly was held, have
been described as a filthy hole with no light, no fresh air, and
a dungeon that was never cleaned. Prisoners often went mad;
almost everyone who entered died there.

These are the conditions in which Paul was faithful to his
charge at the end of his life. Verse 8 begins by looking back
to the challenge of verses 6–7. In light of being given a spirit
"of power and love and discipline," Paul charged Timothy,
"Therefore *do not be ashamed* (vv. 8, 12, 16 NKJV) of the

testimony of our Lord or of me His prisoner." Paul is quick to point out that he is not Rome's prisoner but the Lord's. I am here because he put me here. I am here to suffer for his gospel and to do so by the power of God. In that suffering there should be no shame! No shame of Christ (a crucified criminal), the Lord Jesus, the Messiah King. No shame of his gospel, which is the power of God unto salvation (Rom. 1:16). No shame of his faithful servant (Paul, a subversive anarchist) who willingly and joyfully put it all on the line for King Jesus.

The same charge laid down by Paul to Timothy, would later characterize the life and ministry of David Brainerd (1718–1747). He was born into a devout Christian home in Haddam, Connecticut. Tragically, he would be nine years old when his father died and fourteen years old when his mother died. He would experience lengthy battles with depression, loneliness, and melancholy that would afflict him most of his life. Tuberculosis would dog him most of his three-year ministry among the Indians. In God's providence Brainerd's journal and diary were edited and published by Jonathan Edwards (1703–1758). Through these writings, the life and ministry of David Brainerd have been preserved.

At the age of twenty-one, on July 12, 1739, as he prepared to enter Yale College and prepare for ministry, he was wonderfully converted to the Christ he would faithfully love and serve for a brief eight years. It is appropriate to quote at length Brainerd's own account of this glorious event:

> I was walking again in the same solitary place, where I was brought to see myself lost and helpless. . . . Here, in a mournful, melancholy state, I was attempting to pray; but found no heart to engage in that or any other duty. . . . Then, as I was walking in a dark thick grove, unspeakable glory seemed to open to the view and

apprehension of my soul. I do not mean any external brightness, for I saw no such thing. . . . It was a new inward apprehension or view that I had of God, such as I never had before, nor anything which had the least resemblance of it.

I stood still, wondered, and admired! I knew that I never had seen before anything comparable to it for excellency and beauty. . . . My soul rejoiced with joy unspeakable to see such a God, such a glorious Divine Being; and I was inwardly pleased and satisfied that He should be God over all for ever and ever. My soul was so captivated and delighted with the excellency, loveliness, greatness, and other perfections of God, that I was even swallowed up in Him.

Thus God, I trust, brought me to a hearty disposition to exalt Him and set Him on the throne, and principally and ultimately to aim at His honor and glory, as King of the universe. I continued in this state of inward joy, peace, and astonishment, till near dark, without any sensible abatement; and then began to think and examine what I had seen; and felt sweetly composed in my mind all the evening following. I felt myself in a new world, and everything about me appeared with a different aspect from what it was wont to do.

At this time, the way of salvation opened to me with such infinite wisdom, suitableness, and excellency, that I wondered I should ever think of any other way of salvation; was amazed that I had not dropped my own contrivances, and complied with this lovely, blessed, and excellent way before. If I could have been saved by my own duties, or any other way that I had formerly contrived, my whole soul would now have refused it. I wondered that all the world did not see and comply with this way of salvation, entirely by the righteousness of Christ.[2]

With such a glorious awakening to the excellency and beauty of Christ, it is no wonder David Brainerd was unashamed of Christ and his gospel. There was no shame of Christ and his gospel in Paul. There was no shame of Christ and his gospel in Brainerd. There must be no shame of Christ and his gospel in us.

Certain of Your Calling as a Gospel Minister (2 Tim. 1:9–11)

Paul was confident in his *salvation* (cf. also v. 12). He was equally confident in his *call to ministry*, both its character and its nature. Note the spiritual progression and spiritual logic to Paul's argument in these verses.

1. God "*has saved us* . . . not according to our works." We did not save ourselves (v. 9 NKJV).
2. God called us "with *a holy calling*." God's call is from a holy God and unto a holy life (v. 9 NKJV).
3. This holy calling is "*according to his own purpose and grace*." God sets the agenda for our lives and it is by his grace that we live out his plan for our lives (v. 9 NKJV).
4. This grace was "*given to us in Christ Jesus before time began*." The preexistent Christ set in motion his amazing grace for our salvation and service in eternity past (v. 9 NKJV).
5. This grace has been revealed in space and time, in history, "*by the appearing of our Savior Jesus Christ*" (v. 10 NKJV).
6. The amazing nature of this grace is seen in the fact that the Christ who gives it has "*abolished death*" and

"brought life and immortality to light through the gospel."
No wonder grace is amazing, and no wonder Paul is
not ashamed of the gospel (v. 10 NKJV).

7. With this gospel of the incomparable Christ our Savior
    Paul was appointed to a threefold assignment for the
    nations: (1) *preacher* (herald), (2) *apostle* (missionary)
    and (3) *teacher* (v. 11 NKJV).[3]

Brainerd had the same certainty of God's call and God's
grace as did the apostle Paul. In fact, it was all that kept him
going at particular points in his life. In a letter to his brother
on January 2, 1744, Brainerd wrote, "We should always look
upon ourselves as God's servants, placed in God's world to do
His work; and accordingly labor faithfully for Him. . . . Let it
then be your great concern, thus to devote yourself and your
all to God."[4]

Brainerd was convinced of his call, even if he was not sure
of the same for others. Brainerd enrolled at Yale in 1739. He
was at the top of his class and on his way to graduating with
honors. However, in the winter of 1741, after the fall com-
mencement address given by Jonathan Edwards, an address
entitled "The Distinguishing Marks of a Work of the Spirit
of God," an address not well received by the more reserved
administration, a freshman overheard Brainerd say in a private
conversation of Yale's tutor Chauncey Whittlesey, "I do not
believe he has any more grace than this chair I lean upon."[5]
He was also accused of saying he was surprised that Rector
Thomas Clap "did not drop dead for fining scholars that followed Mr. Tennent."[6] Refusing to publicly apologize, though
he confessed his guilt, Brainerd was expelled from school.
He would later write a letter of public apology and plead to
be forgiven and allowed to graduate. Jonathan Edwards and
others also made appeals on his behalf but all to no avail. He

was never readmitted. He never graduated. Humbled? Yes. Humiliated? No doubt. Denied his calling as a gospel minister? Never! After being denied his degree, Brainerd said, "God sees fit to deny it."[7]

Brainerd often thought deeply about his holy calling and appointment as a preacher, missionary, and teacher. A few excerpts from his diary make this clear:[8]

Monday, June 25, 1744

Was something better in health than of late; was able to spend a considerable part of the day in prayer and close studies. Especially longed for the presence of God in my work and that the poor heathen might be converted. And in evening prayer my faith and hope in God were much raised. To an eye of reason, everything that respects the conversion of the heathen is as dark as midnight; and yet I cannot but hope in God for the accomplishment of something glorious among them.

Tuesday, June 26

In prayer my soul was enlarged, and my faith drawn into sensible exercise. Was enabled to cry to God for my poor Indians; though the work of their conversion appeared impossible with man, yet with God I saw all things were possible . . . I was much assisted in prayer for dear Christian friends and for others that I apprehended to be Christless. But was more especially concerned for the poor heathen and those of my own charge. Was enabled to be instant in prayer for them and hoped that God would bow the heavens and come down for their salvation. It seemed to me there could be no impediment sufficient to obstruct that glorious work, seeing the living God, as I strongly hoped, was engaged for it. . . . Longed that God would purge me more that I might be as a chosen vessel to bear His name among the heathens. Continued in this frame till I dropped asleep.

Thursday, June 28

Spent the morning in reading several parts of the Holy Scripture, and in fervent prayer for my Indians that God would set up His kingdom among them and bring them into His Church. . . . My great concern was for the conversion of the heathen to God; and the Lord helped me to plead with Him for it. Towards noon, rode up to the Indians in order to preach to them. While going, my heart went up to God in prayer for them; could freely tell God He knew that the cause was not mine which I was engaged in, but it was His own cause and it would be for His glory to convert the poor Indians.

Lord's Day, July 1

In the morning, was perplexed with wandering vain thoughts; was much grieved, judged and condemned myself before God. . . . Thus also after I came to the Indians my mind was confused. I felt nothing sensibly of that sweet reliance on God that my soul has been comforted with in days past. Spent the forenoon in this posture of mind and preached to the Indians without any heart.

In the afternoon, I felt still barren when I began to preach, and after about half an hour I seemed to myself to know nothing and to have nothing to say to the Indians; but soon after I found in myself a spirit of love, and warmth, and power, to address the poor Indians. God helped me to plead with them to "turn from all the vanities of the heathen to the living God." I am persuaded the Lord touched their consciences for I never saw such attention raised in them before. And when I came away from them, I spent the whole time, while I was riding to my lodgings three miles distant, in prayer and praise to God.

After I rode more than two miles, *it came into my mind to dedicate myself to God again, which I did with great solemnity and unspeakable satisfaction. Especially gave up myself to him renewedly in the work of the ministry. And this I did by divine grace, I hope, without any expectation or reserve; not in the least shrinking back from any difficulties that might attend this great and blessed work. I seemed to be most free, cheerful and full in this dedication of myself. My whole soul cried: "Lord, to Thee I dedicate myself! Oh, accept of me and let me be Thine forever. Lord, I desire nothing else, I desire nothing more. Oh, come, come, Lord, accept a poor worm. 'Whom have I in heaven but Thee? And there is none upon earth, that I desire besides Thee.'"*

After this, was enabled to praise God with my whole soul that He had enabled me to devote and consecrate all my powers to Him in this solemn manner. *My heart rejoiced in my particular work as a missionary; rejoiced in my necessity of self-denial in many respects.*

Friday, July 6

Awoke this morning in the fear of God. . . . I am, of late, most of all concerned for ministerial qualifications and the conversion of the heathen. Last year, I longed to be prepared for a world of glory and speedily to depart out of this world; but of late all my concern almost is for the conversion of the heathen, and for that end I long to live.

But blessed be God, I have less desire to live for any of the pleasures of the world, than ever I had. *I long and love to be a pilgrim, and want grace to imitate the life, labors and sufferings of Paul among the heathen. And when I long for holiness now it is not so much for myself as formerly; but rather that thereby I may become an "able minister of the New Testament," especially to the heathen.*

Brainerd's delight and certainty in Christ, "who has saved us and called us with a holy calling, not according to our works, but according to His own purpose and grace" (v. 9 NKJV), is evident in each entry of his journal. Only by this joyful certainty in his calling as a gospel minister did Brainerd labor and suffer faithfully among the Indians. His continual concern for the lost souls of Indians was driven by a deep dependence on Christ and conviction that the gospel was the power to salvation. These realities deepened Brainerd's certainty in his calling, which deepened his faithfulness to his task. Following the pattern of the life and ministry of Paul, Brainerd challenges us to become "able ministers of the New Testament," certain of our calling to be gospel ministers.[9]

Willingness to suffer for the sake of Christ (*2 Tim. 1:8, 12*)

Twice in this paragraph Paul speaks of suffering. In verse 8 he invites Timothy to join him in suffering for the gospel. In verse 12 he informs us he has suffered for his ministry as a preacher, apostle, and teacher. The phrase "for this reason" looks back to verse 11 and shows that it was for the sake of the ministry to which he had been called that he suffered for the sake of Christ. One can also consult 2 Corinthians 11:23–33 for a lengthy and detailed description of just a portion of what Paul suffered for the sake of his Savior. And, it was extensive and it was intense. And, it made it all the more possible for God to put on display his amazing power and his amazing grace.

Once more David Brainerd walked in the footsteps of his apostolic example and mentor. This time it was by his willingness to suffer for the sake of Christ. Fred Barlow put things in perspective when he writes:

> By almost every standard known to modern missionary boards, David Brainerd would have been rejected as a missionary candidate. He was tubercular—died of that disease at twenty-nine—and from his youth was frail and sickly. He never finished college, being expelled from Yale for criticizing a professor and for his interest and attendance in meetings of the "New Lights," a religious organization. He was prone to be melancholy and despondent. Yet this young man, who would have been considered a real risk by any present-day mission board, became a missionary to the American Indians and, in the most real sense, "the pioneer of modern missionary work."[10]

It is of providential import to note God's protective hand on young David as he pursued the missionary assignment given to him by God. Brainerd's first journey to what is called the "Forks of the Delaware" resulted in a miracle of God that preserved his life and revered him among the Indians as a "prophet of God." Encamped at the outskirts of the Indian settlement, Brainerd planned to enter the Indian community the next morning to preach to them the gospel of Christ. Unknown to him, his every move was being watched by warriors who had been sent out to kill him. F. W. Boreham records the incident:

> But when the braves drew closer to Brainerd's tent, they saw the paleface on his knees. And as he prayed, suddenly a rattlesnake slipped to his side, lifted up its ugly head to strike, flicked its forked tongue almost in his face, and then without any apparent reason, glided swiftly away into the brushwood. "The Great Spirit is with the paleface!" the Indians said; and thus they accorded him a prophet's welcome.[11]

On April 1, 1743, Brainerd's ministry in Delaware was put on hold when he traveled to Stockbridge, Massachusetts, to begin his ministry to the Mohegan Indians. Through the spring months he lived with a Scottish man and slept on a bed of straw. He traveled a mile and a half each day to be able to preach to the Indians, and he struggled daily with depression, loneliness, illness, and physical discomfort. His diary entry on May 18, 1743, remarks:

> My circumstances are such, that I have no comfort of any kind but what I have in God. I live in the most lonesome wilderness; have but one single person to converse with, that can speak English. Most of the talk

I hear is either Highland Scotch or Indian. I have no fellow Christian to whom I might unbosom myself or lay open my conversation about heavenly things and join in social prayer. I live poorly with regard to the comforts of life. Most of my diet consists of boiled corn, hasty-pudding, etc. I lodge on a bundle of straw, my labor is hard and extremely difficult, and I have little appearance of success, to comfort me.[12]

Brainerd would then live alone in a wigwam through most of the summer, and finally, on July 30, 1743, he moved into a hut he had built for himself. In March 1744 Brainerd was given a chance to leave the wilderness and become the pastor of the church in East Hampton, Long Island. By this time, however, his devotion as a missionary to the Indians far outweighed his desire for a comfortable position, and he chose to stay. On May 1, 1744, however, he received orders to move to his original commission with the Indians in Pennsylvania. Thus, the Mohegan Indians were left under the care of a man named John Sergeant, while Brainerd went back to the "Forks of Delaware."

Upon his arrival in Delaware, Brainerd was greatly discouraged at the state of the Indians. They had been scattered into the wilderness by land-hungry whites; and, though they seemed open to Christianity, they were leery of listening to any white people. Nevertheless, he began preaching in turn to both the Indians and a nearby settlement of Irish. Although the Indians there rejected some of their old ways, they did not put their hope in Christ as a Savior. Brainerd was discouraged by this and did not think that his efforts in the Forks of Delaware were any success. In an attempt to find more success and reach more Indians, he took two trips to the Susquehanna River. Although Indians there had some interest in the gospel he was preaching, Brainerd still found little tangible success in his work. In addition, he became ill during his second journey to the Susquehanna. On several occasions he expected that he would die.

During this time Brainerd became increasingly reliant on God's working on the Indians before he would have any success. He described this in his June 27, 1744, diary entry: "My soul seemed to rely wholly upon God for success, in the diligent and faithful use of means. Saw, with greatest certainty, that the arm of the Lord must be revealed for the help of these poor heathen, if ever they were delivered from the bondage of the powers of darkness."[13] His desire to see the Indians saved grew deeper than it had ever been. On July 23 of the same summer, he wrote: "Had sweet resignation for the divine will and desired nothing so much as the conversion of the heathen to God, and that His kingdom might come in my own heart and the hearts of others."[14]

On June 19, 1745, Brainerd left the Forks of Delaware and went to Crossweeksung, New Jersey, where he would find the great success he had been searching for.[15] As in Pennsylvania, he found on his arrival that the Indians were scattered throughout the land. Unlike before, however, they offered no objections to his preaching and began to quickly gather others to hear the message. At the end of July, during a return visit to the Forks of Delaware, a major breakthrough occurred in Brainerd's ministry: his interpreter, Moses Tautomy, and his wife were saved and baptized. When Brainerd returned to Crossweeksung in August, the Indians were eagerly awaiting him. That month, only six weeks after his first visit to Crossweeksung, Brainerd witnessed a spiritual awakening among the Indians. He was greatly encouraged as many came to a saving knowledge of Christ and many more traveled great distances to hear his message.

Brainerd took this opportunity immediately to begin discipling a new community of believers. He began baptizing those who showed evidence of their salvation, and throughout the fall he met with Indians individually to give them more teaching. On December 21, 1745, he began giving catechetical lectures to those who were ready for even deeper discipleship. On January 31, 1746, a schoolmaster arrived and began teaching children during the day and adults in the evenings. That spring he took a huge step in his ministry by moving the Indians from Crossweeksung to Cranberry, New Jersey, so they could live close to one another in a permanent community and be taught more easily. Less than a year after his arrival, Brainerd had a congregation of over 130 Christian Indians under his watch care. Concerning them he wrote:

> I know of no assembly of Christians where there seems to be so much of the presence of God, where brotherly love so much prevails, and where I should so much delight in the public worship of God, in general, as in my own congregation; although not more than nine months ago, they were worshipping devils and dumb idols under the power of pagan darkness and superstition. Amazing change this! Effected by nothing less than divine power and grace![16]

Tragically, in the fall of 1746, Brainerd's illness began to overcome him. His diary is full of entries about how weak he was and how hard it was to continue his ministry in his physical condition. Consequently he left the Indians in November and traveled to New England, where he was cared for by friends. In March 1747 he returned for what would be his last visit to the Indians before his death. By this time he was depressed by his sickness and even looked forward to death. On May 19,

1747, Brainerd moved into Jonathan Edwards's home in New Hampton, where he would spend the last nineteen weeks of his life under the care of Edwards's daughter, Jerusha. Finally, what he referred to in his diary as "that glorious day" came; he died of tuberculosis on October 9, 1747, at the age of twenty-nine. He was indeed willing to suffer for Christ. As a result, in a world much different from ours and by means of a ministry of only a few years, hundreds of Indians were born into the kingdom of God.

Unsurpassing Confidence in Your Security in Christ (*2 Tim. 1:12*)

Death has a way of putting things in perspective. In his famous Resolutions, Jonathan Edwards wrote: "6) Resolved, To live with all my might, while I do live. 7) Resolved, Never to do anything, which I should be afraid to do, if it were the last hour of my life. 9) Resolved, To think much on all occasions of my own dying, and of the common circumstances which attend death. 17) Resolved, That I will live so as I shall wish I had done when I come to die."[17]

Paul knew he was at life's end. He was in the twilight of life; and though many things were uncertain, one thing he knew for sure: "I know whom I have *believed* and am *persuaded* that *He* (not me) is able to keep what I have committed to Him until that Day."[18] Paul has placed his life, his eternal destiny in the hands of a sovereign God, a God he was confident would keep him no matter what and no matter when. Come life or death, he was secure in the God who is able.

At the end of his life, David Brainerd had the same assurances as Paul. Dying in the home of Jonathan Edwards, cared for by his daughter Jerusha, the evidence pointing to the strong possibility they had fallen in love, Brainerd would write, just days before his death (most if not all his thoughts being dictated to others):

Friday, October 2

My soul was this day, at turns, sweetly set on God. I longed to be with Him that I might behold His glory. I felt sweetly disposed to commit all to Him, even my dearest friends, my dearest flock, my absent brother, and all my concerns for time and eternity. Oh, that His kingdom might come in the world; that they might all love and glorify Him, for what He is in Himself; and that the blessed Redeemer might "see of the travail of his soul, and be satisfied"! Oh, come, Lord Jesus, come quickly! Amen.[19]

In commenting on the last days of Brainerd's life, his friend and mentor, Jonathan Edwards said:[20]

On the morning of the next day, being Lord's Day, October 4, as my daughter Jerusha (who chiefly attended him) came into the room, he looked on her very pleasantly, and said: "Dear Jerusha, are you willing to part with me? I am quite willing to part with you. I am willing to part with you; I am willing to part with all my friends; I am willing to part with my dear brother John, although I love him the best of any creature living. I have committed him and all my friends to God and can leave them with God. Though, if I had thought I should not see you and be happy with you in another world, I could not bear to part with you. But we shall spend a happy eternity together." In the evening, as one came into the room with a Bible in her hand, he expressed himself thus: "Oh, that dear Book! that lovely Book! I shall soon see it opened! The mysteries that are in it, and the mysteries of God's providence, will be all unfolded!"

On Tuesday, October 6, he lay, for a considerable time, as if he were dying. At which time, he was heard to utter, in broken whispers, such expressions as these: "He will come, He will not tarry. I shall soon be in glory. I shall soon glorify God with the angels."

Thursday, October 8, he was in great distress and agonies of body; and for the greater part of the day was much disordered as to the exercise of his reason. . . . He told me it was impossible for any to conceive of the distress he felt in his breast. He manifested much concern lest he should dishonor God by impatience under his extreme agony; which was such that he said the thought of enduring it one minute longer was almost insupportable.

Notwithstanding his bodily agonies, the interest of Zion lay still with great weight on his mind; the great importance of the work of the ministry.

Towards day, his eyes fixed; and he continued lying immovable till about six o'clock in the morning, and then expired on Friday, October 9, 1747, when his soul, as we may well conclude, was received by his dear Lord and Master as an eminently faithful servant, into that state of perfection of holiness and fruition of God, which he had so often and so ardently longed for; and was welcomed by the glorious assembly in the upper world, as one peculiarly fitted to join them in their blessed employ and enjoyment.

Since this, it has pleased a holy and sovereign God to take away this my dear child [Jerusha] by death, on the fourteenth of February, next following; after a short illness of five days, in the eighteenth year of her age. She was a person of much the same spirit with Mr. Brainerd. She had constantly taken care of and attended him in his sickness for nineteen weeks before his death, devoting herself to it with great delight because she looked on him as an eminent servant of Jesus Christ.

In this time, he had much conversation with her on the things of religion; and in his dying state, often expressed to us, her parents, his great satisfaction concerning her true piety and his confidence that he should meet her in heaven; and his high opinion of her, not only as a true Christian, but a very emi-nent saint; one whose soul was uncommonly fed and entertained with things that appertain to the most spiritual, experimental, and distinguishing parts of religion; and one who, by the temper of her mind, was fitted to deny herself for God and to do good, beyond any young woman whatsoever that he knew of. She had manifested a heart uncommonly devoted to God in the course of her life, many years before her death; and said on her deathbed, that she had not seen one minute for several years, wherein she desired to live one minute longer, for the sake of any other good in life, but doing good, living to God, and doing what might be for His glory.

This is how Brainerd lived and how he died. This is how the young girl he loved lived and died. No wonder he wrote, "Oh, how precious is time! And how guilty it makes me feel when I think I have trifled away and misapproved it, or neglected to fill up each part of it with duty to the utmost of my ability and capacity."[21]

Conclusion

David Brainerd died in 1747 in the home of Jonathan Edwards. His ministry to the Indians was contemporary with Wesley, Whitefield, and Edwards as they ministered to the English-speaking people during the period called in English and American history the "Great Awakening." Brainerd's centuries-spanning influence for revival is positive proof God can and will use any vessel, no matter how fragile and frail, if he or she is only radically devoted to the Savior!

J. M. Sherwood said that David Brainerd's story "has done more to develop and mold the spirit of modern missions, and to fire the heart of the Christian Church, than that of any man since the apostolic age."[22] He never left New England, but through those he inspired he has spoken to India, Burma, New Zealand, Persia, and Ecuador just to name a few.

When asked, "What can be done to revive the word of God where it has decayed?" John Wesley said, "Let every preacher read carefully the life of David Brainerd."[23] We have looked at this man and his life as it unfolded in the shadow of the pattern of the apostle Paul. F. W. Boreham described him as, "a man in a million."[24] It is wisely said, "He lives long who lives well." By that measurement David Brainerd lived long. My hope and prayer is that we will live long too.

CHAPTER 8

God's Chariot of Fire:
The Life of Missionary Eric Liddell and the Race He Ran

Hebrews 12:1–3

 He was born to missionary parents in China. He would die in the same country living out that same missionary calling. And yet his faithful service to King Jesus is often eclipsed by his extraordinary gift as a runner and his brilliant performance in the 1924 Olympics in Colombes Stadium in Paris, where he won the Gold Medal and set the world and Olympic record in the four-hundred-meter race.

Eric Liddell's career as a world champion runner was made famous in the 1982 movie *Chariots of Fire*, a film that was nominated for seven Academy Awards and won four, including best picture. There he is accurately portrayed as a man fully surrendered to God whose conviction concerning the Lord's Day led him to refuse to run on Sunday during the Olympics. However, there is so much more to this man whose life was all too brief. He would die of an inoperable brain tumor at the age of forty-three.

The Bible often uses the images of athletics to teach us important truths about the Christian life. In 1 Corinthians 9:26 and 2 Corinthians 4:9, God's Word compares the Christian life to boxing. In Ephesians 6:12 it is wrestling. But in 1 Corinthians 9:26; 2 Timothy 4:7; and Hebrews 12:1–3 the analogy is that of a race. Here in the book of Hebrews the comparison clearly is to a long distance race because we are told to run with "endurance." In fact some form of the word *endurance* is found in each of the first three verses of Hebrews 12. If the Bible were being written today, the writer might allude to a marathon. After all it is a 26.2-mile race (42.19 kilometers) and the longest run in the modern Olympics.

So the Christian life can be compared to a long-distance race, not a sprint. That means we need both a different training and a different strategy if we are to run well and finish well and hear from our heavenly Father, "Well done, good and faithful servant" (Matt. 25:23 NKJV).

Hebrews 12:1–3 contains three clear and overarching themes for how we are to run the race. We will see each of these beautifully illustrated in the life of the man Eric Liddell, a man who would write: "Jesus' life is the most beautiful life there has ever been. . . . They [the disciples] failed him at his death, but with the resurrection and Pentecost they awoke to the meaning of the message he had been trying to give them, and went out to conquer the world."[1] Eric Liddell would gladly follow in their footsteps.

Find Encouragement As You Run (*Heb. 12:1*)

We are told to be encouraged as we run the race of the Christian life. Why? Because "we also have such a large crowd of witnesses surrounding us" (HCSB). The imagery is that of the coliseum or stadium. The grandstands are filled to capacity, and we are on the track running the race. Some believe the text is teaching that people in heaven are looking down and watching, but I don't think this is what the passage means. Rather it is encouraging us to look around because we are not running by ourselves. There are no Lone Rangers in this race. Further, the word "therefore" is there for a reason. It points us back to chapter 11 and God's Hall of Faith. Here we find men and women who have already run the race and crossed the finish line. Their lives are recorded to help us so that we "won't grow weary and lose heart" (12:3 HCSB). God gives us heroes of the faith to encourage and inspire us as we run. This is one of the reasons I so love missionary biographies. They always encourage me.

Eric Liddell certainly had heroes like this in his own parents. He was born in Tienstsin (Tianjin), China, on January 16, 1902, as the second son of godly and faithful missionary parents, James and Mary Liddell. They were strongly devoted to evangelical Christianity and answered God's call to go to China through the London Missionary Society (LMS). His parents would, like their son, serve in China during extremely turbulent and dangerous times. They would also serve with grace, distinction, and resolve. They would serve during the Boxer Rebellion when more than two hundred missionaries would be murdered. James would serve in a rural area where eighty churches were destroyed and hundreds of Chinese Christians killed. And yet Eric's father would say to the LMS, "I would gladly undertake the duties pertaining to a real pioneer situation."[2] And he did! The champion that Eric Liddell would become he saw first in his own father and mother.

His close friend and biographer D. P. Thomson gave an address in 1946 following Eric's untimely death in China. He raised the question, "What was his secret?" Here was his answer, "It was first of all the home from which he came. No one who knew Liddell's father and mother, no one who had been a guest in their home, who had sensed its atmosphere and its outlook, and had become aware of the spirit which permeated it, could be in any doubt about that. Home was the first great formative influence in the making and shaping of Eric Liddell, as it was of so many. It was there that he got both his ideals and his inspirations."[3]

Proverbs 22:6 says, "Train up a child in the way he should go, and when he is old he will not depart from it" (NKJV). This was true in the life of Eric Liddell. He caught the "missionary bug" as a child, and it stayed with him all his life.

In 1932, after his first missionary furlough, Eric was interviewed in Canada by journalist R. E. Knowles, who asked Eric, "Are you glad you gave your life to missionary work? Don't you miss the limelight, the rush, the frenzy, the cheers, the rich red wine of victory?" Eric's reply was gracious but to the point, "Oh well, of course it's natural for a chap to think over all that sometimes, but I'm glad I'm in the work I'm engaging in now. A fellow's life counts for more at this than the other. Not a corruptible crown, but an incorruptible, you know."[4]

Perhaps David Guest said it best, "Eric Liddell, rugby international and Olympic gold medalist, universally admired for his high character, happy humor and for his Christianity, brushed fame calmly aside to return as a missionary to China, where he had been born."[5] The encouragement Eric received as a child from his parents to "seek first the kingdom of God and His righteousness" (Matt. 6:33 NKJV) never left him. Fame and fortune did not motivate him. Surrender and obedience to the will of God did, something he saw so clearly and consistently in the lives of his mom and dad. None of us who are parents should ever underestimate our words or our example to our children. How often they walk in our footsteps, especially in the areas where we encourage them. The making of a champion for Christ may be in the works!

Focus on the Essentials as You Run (*Heb. 12:1*)

Any kind of race requires both training and a strategy. For a long-distance race endurance or perseverance is a must. For the devoted follower of King Jesus whose goal is to run well and finish well, verse 1 provides three critical keys for success. They are simple but essential. To neglect even one is to ensure a much more difficult race, if not failure. We must run this race *cleanly* ("lay aside every weight"), *with confidence* ("lay aside . . . the sin which so easily ensnares us") and *consistently* ("with endurance"). Each of these essentials is beautifully illustrated in the life of Eric Liddell.

Few men ever ran less encumbered, with greater faith and consistency of life than did "the flying Scotsman."[6] Eric was always a good student, but he was a great athlete. He was also quiet and shy. However, as his fame spread because of his athletic ability both as a rugby player and runner, D. P. Thomson saw an opportunity for the gospel. He approached Eric with an invitation to speak about his faith in Christ. This was in April 1923. Eric agreed reluctantly but then began second-guessing his decision.

Providentially on that very day he received a letter from China (he was now living in Scotland in boarding school as was the custom, especially for sons of missionaries during those years) from his sister Jenny. Mailed weeks earlier, she closed the letter with Isaiah 41:10, "Fear not for I am with thee, be not dismayed for I am thy God; I will strengthen thee, yea I will help thee; yea I will uphold thee with the right hand of my righteousness." Eric was emboldened by this and pressed on in faith that this was God's plan. And it was. God would bless his speaking and use this soft-spoken and shy man as a proclaimer of the gospel until his race was finished.

Crowds would often flock to hear, in part, because of the transparent humility and sincerity of this incredible champion. He laid aside the weight of fear, placed his trust in God alone, and would speak of Christ whenever and wherever he was invited regardless of the crowd or context.

Eric would later write Thomson telling him he had become a changed man since he invited him to bear public witness to Christ and that a new joy had come into his life. Later in his personal journey, he would refer to this turning point in his life and write:

> I was brought up in a Christian home where the sto-
> ries of the Bible were often told and became familiar
> to me. In school, the stories of the Bible and the teach-
> ings of Christ were placed before me. The beauty of
> the Christian life began to appeal to me. The time
> came when the appeal of Christ became more per-
> sonal and I began to realize that it was going to affect
> my life. In this experience of Christ there was a sense
> of sin but that was not nearly so great as the sense
> of being called to do a piece of work for which I was
> absolutely unqualified.
>
> My whole life had been one of keeping out of pub-
> lic duties but the leading of Christ seemed now to
> be in the opposite direction, and I shrank from going
> forward. At this time I finally decided to put it all on

Christ—after all if He called me to do it, then He would have to supply the necessary power. In going forward the power was given me. Since then the consciousness of being an active member of the Kingdom of Heaven has been very real. New experiences of the Grace of God, sense of sin, wonders of the Bible have come from time to time. All these fresh experiences have given me fresh visions of our Lord.[7]

Run Cleanly

We are challenged to "lay aside every weight" (Heb. 12:1–2). To say it another way, we are to take off, remove, and put away any excess baggage. Anything that would weigh us down and slow us down and keep us from running our best for Jesus is to be discarded. Eric Liddell well understood some of the weights that could hinder us from running well for Jesus.

To avoid these he advised four tests we should regularly ask ourselves: (1) Am I *truthful*? (2) Am I *honest*? (3) Am I *pure*? (4) Am I *selfish*? And, there would be other weights Liddell would identify he knew would hinder us in running the race well and would especially be harmful to the missionary calling. Note just a sampling he would address:

Prejudices—I believe it is God's will that the whole world should be without any barriers of race, colour, class, or anything else that breaks the spirit of fellowship.[8]

Distraction—*Every Christian should live a God-guided life.* If you are not guided by God, you will be guided by someone or something else.[9]

Rebellion—Surrender means the end of the great rebellion of our wills.[10]

Disobedience—Sin is anything we know we should do but won't or don't do. It is therefore disobedience.[11]

Persecution—The only way to face persecution is to rejoice. Any other way of facing it fails to come out victorious. The apostles rejoiced "that they were counted worthy to suffer shame for his name (Acts 5:41 NKJV).[12]

Lordship—To speak of Jesus as Lord means that I give him the control of my will. . . . I say "Lord Jesus," meaning Jesus is now Lord of my life to lead and dictate. My greatest joy is just to do what pleases him.[13]

Unexpected hardships—Circumstances may appear to wreck our lives and God's plans, but God *is not helpless among the ruins.*[14]

Run with Confidence

We are also challenged to lay aside "the sin" that so easily ensnares or entangles us. I call this "the octopus of the Christian life," and I believe it is the same sin for everyone: the sin of unbelief. I think this is the correct interpretation because Hebrews 11 precedes Hebrews 12, and it is all about faith. In fact verse 6 warns us that "without faith it is impossible to please [God]." And the definite article "the" before the word "sin" in our text, I believe, specifies a particular sin. Unbelief is often a seductive sin, especially for a Christian. It is what I call the "I need Jesus plus" trap. Once we add anything to Jesus for our salvation or our sanctification, we have run into the world of unbelief. We must seek a radical faith and dependence in God that can say like Job, "Even if He [God] kills me, I will hope in Him" (Job 13:15).

Eric Liddell grasped this truth well. He spoke of "two ways of living." One was the life lived by the law that cannot change us. The other was a life lived by faith "where righteousness comes by grace on God's side, and by trust and confidence in Christ on our side."[15] Such faith would lead to what Eric referred to as "victorious living," a favorite theme of his. Such victory, he said quite simply, *"comes by a practical confidence in God and acting on the promises he has given us."* And the keys? (1) "Keep your eyes off yourself and on your Savior." (2) "Keep your eyes off yourself and on God's strength." (3) "Fear comes by looking at oneself or others instead of looking at Jesus." (4) "To believe means to act on what in your heart you know is right. Faith acts—victory follows."[16] The bottom line: "Trust absolutely: remember, God asks faithfulness—victory follows."[17]

Run Consistently

Third, we are called to "run with endurance the race that lies before us." Shooting-star Christians who burn bright for a night and then vanish into the midnight darkness bring little glory to God and do not serve well the body of Christ. I believe our Lord is teaching us in this verse it is not how high you jump that is important but how long you keep running.

Eric Liddell would teach that the key to perseverance or endurance was found in one of his favorite components of the Christian life: radical surrender. It would be the last word he would ever speak. It would be a commitment he would honor throughout his life of sacrificial service to Christ.

"God's will is only revealed to us step by step. He reveals more as we obey what we know. Surrender means we are prepared to follow his will step by step as it is revealed to us, no matter what."[18]

He would later add, "God does not say that because you believe in him, he will keep you from hardship and suffering. He says, if you trust him, he will strengthen you to meet all the experiences of life in a conquering spirit. You will have secret resources of power to call on when they are needed."[19]

Follow the Example as You Run (Heb. 12:2–3)

Eric Liddell loved, adored, worshipped, and served passionately King Jesus. He wrote in his discipleship book, "I believe in Jesus the Christ, the Son of God, as Example, Lord and Saviour."[20] Each of these is found in the book of Hebrews, but it is the theme of Christ as our example that we find emphasized here. It is also one Eric would address at some length in his only book *The Disciplines of the Christian Life*. There he would write: "Have a great aim—have a high standard—make Jesus your ideal. Be like him in character. Be like him in outlook and attitude towards God and man. . . . Make him an ideal not merely to be admired but also to be followed."[21] But having him as an example or ideal was not enough, and Eric well understood this. Thus he would add: "I find I need more than an ideal: I need a Saviour to save me from the *guilt of sin*; to save me from the *power of sin*. I need a Saviour whose *grace is sufficient to enable me to live a life of unselfish service and love.*"[22] Thus he would add as an aid to our daily quiet time, "*Accept Christ into your life for today*, with all his qualities of outgoing love, honesty, purity, and unselfishness, and with his passion to do God's will. Where you failed yesterday to measure up to Christ's standards, be honest about it; accept promptly God's forgiveness and release in Christ; *get up and go on* in his strength."[23]

Look to Jesus (Heb. 12:2)

Verse 2 calls us to keep our eyes on Jesus as we run. "Keeping" is a good rendering of a present-tense participle.

The idea is to go forward and move ahead gluing your eyes on Jesus so that you are not distracted by anything else. Like a faithful mate in marriage, we are to have eyes only for Jesus. Why? The text tells us he is "the source and perfector of our faith" (HCSB). Jesus *saves* us, and Jesus *sustains* us all the way to the end! He gets us in the race and he will get us to the finish line. And he is more than sufficient for this task because he also ran in a race, a race that took him to the cross where he paid in full the penalty of sin as our substitute. This death was a joy to him, one he willingly endured for the glory of his Father and the good of sinners, one in which he despised the shame of it, and one that resulted in his being seated, exalted, at the right hand of God's throne (cf. Ps. 2; 110).

Eric would see a connection between looking to Jesus and the Christian grace of humility: "*Humility looks at its sins* (self-examination) but also *looks beyond them* to the Savior from sin and casts itself upon his mercy. . . . *Humility is powerful*, for it is based on the sense of being absolutely dependent on the grace of God."[24]

Eric was also captivated by both the cross and the resurrection of Jesus. He would write:

> *Jesus is the Son of God. The stupendous mystery of the cross has now to be revealed. . . . The cross must be. No cross. No crown. . . .* This cross [is] where men saw revealed the magnitude of God's love and the awfulness of their own sin. Nor was that all, for there was the Lamb of God taking away the sin of the world. *Forgiveness!* O blessed word to those bowed down by the guilt of sin. . . . The cross is not the end; there follows the victory of the resurrection. . . . The resurrection has a meaning for life. *It means the possibility of new life here and now, a risen life, a new quality of*

being. Life! Eternal life! . . . Christ has risen! No wonder the hymns about the resurrection resound with
hallelujahs, for his resurrection brings to everyone the
victory of God in life and death. New life! New joy!
New hope![25]

Think about Jesus (Heb. 12:3)

Verse 3 says "Consider Him who endured such hostility
from sinners against Himself" (HCSB). The word *consider* is
an imperative, a word of command. It means to study, meditate upon, carefully analyze. Think on the passion of the
Christ "so that you won't grow weary and lose heart," (HCSB),
regardless of the circumstances you face. Press on with your
heart and mind fixed on Jesus. You can trust him to get you
home.

Just before Pearl Harbour in 1941, Eric arranged for his
pregnant wife Florence and two daughters to leave China.
He had planned to follow them, but that would never happen. Eric would die in China never seeing his third little girl.
However, this champion for Christ did not despair. He would
not grow weary and lose heart. He would continue to serve
as a faithful missionary until he was sent to an internment
camp in Weihsein in August 1943. There he would continue
to serve King Jesus faithfully and be an inspiration to many,
especially the children who fondly called him Uncle Eric. In
what David Mitchell, a fellow missionary who was imprisoned
with Eric, called, "the squalor of the open cesspools, rats, flies
and disease in the crowded camp, life took on a normal rou-
tine, though without the faithful and cheerful support of Eric
Liddell, many people would never have been able to manage."
Once more David Mitchell raised the question, "What was his
secret?" His answer: "He unreservedly committed his life to

Jesus Christ as his Saviour and Lord. That friendship meant everything to him. By the flickering light of a peanut-oil lamp, early each morning he and a roommate in the men's cramped dormitory studied the Bible and talked with God for an hour. As a Christian, Eric Liddell's desire was to know God more deeply, and as a missionary, to make him known more fully."[26] And this he did both in life and death.

Conclusion

Eric Liddell died in a Japanese internment camp in Weihsien, China, on February 21, 1945, just a few months before the end of World War II. He would be buried there as well. He had an inoperable brain tumor that later was discovered through an autopsy. The nation of Scotland wept. The *Glasgow Evening News* wrote, "Scotland has lost a son who did her proud every hour of his life."[27] Contrary to popular opinion he never said, "God made me fast. And when I run, I feel His pleasure." However, he did say: "We are all missionaries. Wherever we go we either bring people nearer to Christ or we repel them from Christ."[28] Eric Liddell faithfully and consistently did the former, living a life that was a fragrant aroma of the King he loved and served until the very end. If one had any doubts about this, listen to the testimonies of those who knew him best.

David McGavin, General Secretary of the National Bible Society of Scotland:

Eric Liddell was the most Christlike man I ever knew, and there are many who, like me, thank God upon every remembrance of him.[29]

Arnold Bryson, London Missionary Society:

Yesterday a man said to me, "Of all the men I have known, Eric Liddell was the one in whose character and life the spirit of Jesus Christ was pre-eminently manifested." And all of us who were privileged to know him with any intimacy echo this judgment. What was the secret of his consecrated life and far-reaching influence? Absolute surrender to God's Will, as revealed in Jesus Christ. His was a God-controlled life and he followed his Master and Lord with devotion that never flagged and with an intensity of purpose that made men see both the reality and power of true religion.[30]

D. P. Thomson, close friend and first biographer of Eric Liddell:

Never in the years we worked together—in shadow or in sunshine, in times of testing and difficulty, in hours of exhilarating triumph—did I hear him say or know him do anything of which I can imagine Christ would have disapproved. His was the most consistent Christian character, as well as one of the most attractive and winning of personalities of any man I have ever known intimately.

With it all went his unfailing sense of humour—"that smiling face, with the twinkling blue eyes," as the one who knew him best described it—his character, his readiness to help personally at the cost of any inconvenience or self-sacrifice, his wish that others and not he should have the glory when success crowned his efforts, and his intense desire to be ever in the path of obedience to Him to whom he had given his all.

Athlete, evangelist, missionary—friend, husband and father—he has been missed as few men of his generation have been. By multitudes he is remembered with affection and gratitude as one in whose life they saw so much of the strength and beauty of Christ.[31]

Norman Cliff, fellow internee in Weihsien:

Eric Liddell would say, "When you speak of me, give the glory to my Master, Jesus Christ. . . ." He would want us to see the Christ whom he served.[32]

An unknown prostitute from Tientsin who told how Eric put up a shelf for her:

He was the first man to do something for me without asking for a favor in return.[33]

Florence Liddell, his wife:

I feel that Eric and I had as much happiness in our few short years together (not quite 11 years) as many couples have in a whole lifetime and I thank God for the privilege of being Eric's wife. I only hope the children. . . . will take after Eric and follow in their Master's footsteps.[34]

Nurse Annie Buchan was with Eric Liddell as he died. Just before he lapsed into a coma from which he would not awake, he said to her, "Annie, it is surrender." With those as his final words, God's "Chariot of Fire" crossed the finish line and completed his race. It may well be that in his last words he gave us the key to running and finishing well our own race for our Master and King.

So, what is the race God is calling us to run together as his body, the church? I believe Eric Liddell has a word for us as we bring our all too brief survey of his life to an end:

Jesus came to proclaim the kingdom of God, to offer its blessings to those who would take heed, and to instruct people in its obligations and responsibilities. When he left, he committed to the church the duty of carrying on this work. The church is his voice in the world announcing the good news about God, calling men everywhere to repent and inviting them to enter the kingdom. *Every individual in the church shares this responsibility.* We are called to witness. Are we doing it?[35]

CHAPTER 9

The Missionary Psalm:
Beautifully Obeyed in the Life and
Martyrdom of John and Betty Stam

Psalm 67

 "The faithfulness of God is the only certain thing in the world today. We need not fear the result of trusting Him."[1] Those words were penned by John Stam, a young missionary to China, who along with his gifted wife Betty would trust King Jesus all the way to their beheading. They would accept the sovereign results of God in their lives, which came to an untimely end at the tender ages of twenty-eight (Betty) and twenty-seven (John). Missionary Daniel Smith noted: "They were roughly handled, stripped of their outward clothing, painfully bound, and publically beheaded. They died—but not without the comfort and support of the Lord, and not without the light of life shining through the darkest circumstances life could bring."[2]

God indeed made his face to shine upon John and Betty Stam as he promises to those who seek his praise among the nations. Psalm 67 was beautifully fulfilled in their lives and in their deaths. This psalm is part of a collection (Pss. 65–68) that emphasizes God's providence and his concern for Israel, the nations, and all creation (cf. Ps. 66:1, 4, 8). Out of gratitude for God's blessings to his people (vv. 6–7), we are moved to go to "all" (vv. 2, 3, 5, 7) nations and peoples and tell them of his "saving power" (v. 2).

The psalm is rooted in the great Abrahamic covenant in Genesis 12:1–3 and the beautiful Aaronic blessing in Numbers 6:24–26. Its missionary impulse is made clear by a number of observations. First, Hebrews and Gentiles come together to praise and fear God. Second, the "nations" are mentioned three times (vv. 2, 4). Additionally, the "earth" is noted four times (vv. 2, 4, 6, 7). Fourth, the "peoples" are referenced five times (vv. 3–5). Finally, the word "all" appears four times. This anonymous psalmist had an unwavering confidence and conviction that God would be praised by all the peoples of all the nations. John and Betty Stam had it in their heart to be used by God to bring all of this to fruition. No wonder at the tender age of eighteen Betty could write:

> Lord, I give up all my own plans and purposes all my own desires and hopes and accept Thy will for my life. I give myself, my life, my all utterly to Thee to be Thine forever. Fill me and seal me with Thy Holy Spirit. Use me as Thou wilt, send me where Thou wilt and work out Thy whole will in my life at any cost now and forever.[3]

God's Salvation Must Be Known
among the Nations (Ps. 67:1–3)

There are nearly sixty-nine hundred Unreached People Groups with a population of 2.8 billion people (Joshua Project). This means they have little or no access at all to the gospel of Jesus Christ. However, the psalmist prays that the Lord's "way may be known on earth, your saving power among all nations" (v. 2 ESV).

God's saving power was made known in the sending of his missionary Son, Jesus, who declared his mission in Luke 19:10, "For the Son of Man has come to seek and save that which was lost." Dying a bloody death on a Roman cross, he made satisfaction for sins as our penal substitute. God then raised him from the dead and declared that repentance of sin and faith in his Son should be proclaimed to all the nations, fulfilling Psalm 67.

So engulfed in this salvation that he could scarce think of living without it, John Stam wrote to one of his brothers:

> Take away anything I have, but do not take away the sweetness of walking and talking with the King of Glory! It is good to let our thoughts run away with us, sometimes, concerning the greatness of our God and His marvelous kindness toward us. Looking back, what encouragement we find for the future, what wonderful leadings and providence! Oh, bless the Lord, my soul![4]

Now, note three beautiful components or aspects of the salvation we are to proclaim among the nations.

The Nations Must Know of His Mercy (Ps. 67:1)

We serve a God who is gracious, loving, kind, and wonderful. The psalmist begins by praying that God would do three things for his children. The verse echoes Aaron's blessing found in Numbers 6:24–26. First, "be gracious to us" (ESV). God's grace is the source of all His blessings to us in Christ and is completely undeserved and without merit. Second, "Bless us," he asks. Remove the ravaging effects of the curse and fall of Adam (Gen. 3). Rather than pour out on us the wrath and judgment we deserve, abundantly flood us with your favor and goodness. Note the idea of blessing appears three times in our text (vv. 1, 6, 7). Third, "make your face to shine upon us." The idea is, "Lord, look upon us with your pleasure and acceptance." See us clothed in the righteousness of Christ and smile at us with your love and acceptance. I love Proverbs 16:15 in this context, "In the light of a king's face there is life, and his favor is like the clouds that bring the spring rain" (ESV).

John and Betty both knew of God's great mercy. Each was born into a strong and vibrant Christian home. John's father and mother ran the Star of Hope Mission in Paterson, New Jersey, where it was said, "Scores of young people, converted and trained in the Mission, have gone to other fields, at home and abroad, and still the Word of God is being sent out from the old center in no fewer than 40 languages."[5] John would trust Christ at the age of fifteen under the preaching of a blind evangelist who was holding special services at the Mission.[6] Of his passion for Christ he would write: "I would sooner be the most humble Christian, than have all a man could want of earthly things and yet be without Christ. . . . Oh, He is a wonderful Savior and Lord, and a wonderful Master to work for."[7]

Betty was born into a Presbyterian missionary family and raised in China, the place where she and John would be martyred. The godly influence and passion for the nation of her parents was so great that each of their five children served King Jesus as missionaries. Of this remarkable heritage Betty wrote, "All five of us children expected at that time to return to China as missionaries. Our parents never urged it, but it seemed the natural and right thing to do."[8]

God's grace would bring John and Betty together at Moody Bible Institute where they fell in love. Both felt God's leading to China. Betty sailed for China in 1931 at the age of twenty-five. John left the next year. He was also twenty-five. Yes, he married an older woman! By God's providence they would marry on October 25, 1933. They had been separated for a year while on the mission field and would marry the next day after being reunited!

It is worth noting that Betty had prayed and thought long on the man she would marry. In fact, at the tender age of eighteen, this gifted poet would describe the man she believed God had for her. In a poem entitled "My Ideal," the last stanza reads:

> He will not be a rich man,
> He has no earthly hoard;
> His money, time, heart, mind and soul
> Are given to the Lord.
> He'll be a modern Daniel,
> A Joshua, a Paul;
> He will not hesitate to give
> To God his earthly all.
> He'll be, he'll be, my hero—
> A strong-armed fighting man,
> Defender of the Gospel,

And Christian gentleman.
Oh, if he asks a Question,
My answer "Yes" will be!
For I would trust and cherish
Him to eternity.[9]

John and Betty could gladly tell the nations of God's mercy to the nations because they had experienced it so richly in their own lives.

The Nations Must Learn of His Salvation (Ps. 67:2)

As the communist threat was growing in China in the 1930s, many counseled the missionaries to retreat and even return home. John's response was quick and clear, "If we wait til all is peaceful, how shall the present suffering generation hear the Gospel? We have our unalterable commission from Him who gave His life for us—Matthew 28:18–20. The words of a great military leader in this connection give us the true perspective: "Look to your marching orders! How do these read?"[10]

Verse 2 is a beautiful example of Hebrew parallelism where different words affirm the same truth. God's blessings, poured out on his people (v. 1), is for the purpose: "that your way may be known on earth, your saving power among all nations." God blesses us in order that the nations will know personally, intimately, and experientially his ways and experience the power of his salvation. Do not miss what the psalmist is saying. We can and should pray for God's blessings in our lives and do it for the sake of the salvation of the nations! "God, bless me, but not for me—for the use of me for the salvation of all peoples!"

Betty Stam knew something of this truth and, as a young college student, shared her heart in a letter to one of her brothers:

No one can force a single soul, Christian (so-called) or heathen, to turn to Christ. All His followers have to do, all they can do, is to lift up Christ before the world, bring Him into dingy corners and dark places of the earth where He is unknown, introduce Him to strangers, talk about Him to everybody, and live so closely with and in Him that others may see that there really is such a person as Jesus, because some human being proves it by being like Him. That is positively all the Lord asks us to do for Him, because He Himself does the rest. Jesus isn't dead, you see. He is still on earth and in heaven all the time. He's perfectly able to talk with people, and He is more powerful and more perfect even than He was on earth long ago. He is still watching and working for the salvation of the whole world. Only He can't get in touch with any human being until that person asks Him in to talk with him. And no one can ask Him in, if he has never heard of Him. That is where our work comes in—to introduce strangers to Christ; only, on His side, no one is a stranger, for Jesus knows and loves everyone.[11]

On a piece of trampled paper found in their home in Tsingteth following their execution, Betty had penned these words:

Open my eyes, that I may see
This one and that one needing Thee,
Hearts that are dumb, unsatisfied,
Lives that are dead, for whom Christ died.

Open my eyes in sympathy,
Clear into man's deep soul to see;

Wise with Thy wisdom to discern,
And with Thy heart of love to yearn.

Open my eyes in faith, I pray;
Give me the strength to speak today,
Someone to bring, dear Lord, to Thee:
Use me, O Lord, use even me.[12]

The Nations Must Enjoy His Praise (Ps. 67:3)

The blessings of God in salvation always give way to worship, and here all the nations (v. 2), all the peoples (v. 3), praise the great God of our salvation. Verse 3 will be repeated in verse 5. The "peoples" are mentioned five times in verses 3–5. All the peoples: north, south, east and west. All the peoples: black, brown, red, white, and yellow. All the peoples, all 16,689 people groups constituting over seven billion people will praise the God and Father of our Lord Jesus Christ for such a great and incomparable salvation.

John Stam was a much-admired and respected student at Moody Bible Institute. He was chosen by his classmates to give the class address at his graduation. "The Field Is the World" was the title of his historic address. This now famous speech had a powerful and lasting impression. Here is just a portion of it.

In politics, today, men are thinking in terms of international affairs. In business, all the continents are being combed for markets; and even in daily life, every newspaper reader is becoming world conscious. And yet, we, the people of God, have not fully realized that we are to be a testimony to the world. . . . Heathen populations are growing in numbers daily, but we are not reaching them, much less matching their increasing numbers with increased efforts to bring them the Gospel. . . .

Our own civilization also challenges us as Christian workers. This country, once so strong in its Christian testimony, is becoming increasingly godless. . . .

We have been guilty of acting more like the beleaguered garrison of a doomed fortress than like soldiers of our ever-conquering Christ. . . .

Shall we beat a retreat, and turn back from our high calling in Christ Jesus; or dare we advance at God's command, in face of the impossible? . . . Let us remind ourselves that the Great Commission was never qualified by clauses calling for advance only if funds were plentiful and no hardship or self-denial involved. On the contrary, we are told to expect tribulation and even persecution, but with it victory in Christ. . . .

Friends, the task with all its attendant difficulties is enough to fill our hearts with dismay, if we look only to ourselves and our weakness. But the authority in our Master's command to go forward should fill us with joy and the expectation of victory. He knows our weakness and our lack of supplies. He knows the roughness of the way. And His command carries with it the assurance of all we need. . . . The faithfulness of God is the only certain thing in the world today. We need not fear the result of trusting him. . . .

Our way is plain. We must not retrench in any work which we are sure is in His will and for His glory. We dare not turn back because the way looks dark. . . . We must go forward in the face of the impossible, even if we only know the next step. . . .

This bewildering age needs to know that only "the foundation of God standeth sure." Many a man is being torn loose, these days, from the things to which his heart has clung. It is ours to show the incorruptible riches which bank failures and economic conditions cannot reach. It is ours to show, in the salvation of our Lord Jesus Christ, and in personal communion with Him, a joy unspeakable and full of glory that cannot be affected by outside circumstances. . . .

Does it not thrill our hearts to realize that we do not go forward in our own strength? Think of it, God Himself is with us for our Captain! The Lord of Hosts is present in person on every field of conflict, to encourage us and fight with us. With such a Leader, who never lost a battle, or deserted a soldier in distress, or failed to get through the needed supplies, who would not accept the challenge to go forward, "bearing precious seed"?[13]

God's Righteousness Must Be Known among the Nations (Ps. 67:4–5)

Our God is an awesome God who will be known among all the nations. He is also a personal God who takes notice of individual people and is concerned about what goes on in their lives. By invading our world through his people and supremely through his Son, King Jesus, he reveals his character and puts on display his glory for our enjoyment. In verses 4–5 the psalmist notes two particular aspects of his character we should know and share. Indeed these are things we should "gossip about" our God among the nations!

Tell Them He Is a God of Justice (Ps. 67:4)

The nations are encouraged to be glad and sing for joy. Gladness of heart and joyfulness in song should captivate those who have been redeemed by the precious blood of the Lamb, the Lord Jesus.

However, the psalmist would also have us "sing for joy" for two additional reasons. First, God judges the peoples with equity (NIV, "justly"; NKJV, "righteously"). Second, God guides the nations upon earth. "Selah!" Think about that and meditate on it.

The imagery is that of the Shepherd King of Psalm 23 who guides us in the paths of righteousness for his name's sake (v. 3). And our God judges all peoples without partiality or prejudice (cf. Acts 10:34). When we all stand before the judgment bar of God, John Piper well says, "No bribes will be considered, no sophisticated plea-bargaining. All will proceed on the basis of God's unimpeachable righteousness."[14] There is never a "let's make a deal with this God."

Betty Stam, in particular, knew and trusted the guiding hand of this righteous God. Writing to her parents, she said, "I don't know what God has in store for me. I really am willing to be an old-maid missionary, or an old-maid anything else, all my life, if God wants me to. It is as clear as daylight to me that the only worth-while life is one of unconditional surrender to God's will, and of living in His way, trusting His love and guidance."[15]

A year later, after entering college, she would add, "When we consecrate ourselves to God, we think we are making a great sacrifice, and doing lots for Him, when really we are only letting go of some little bitsy trinkets we have been grabbing, and when our hands are empty, He fills them full of His treasure."[16]

Tell Them He Is a God Worthy of Praise (Ps. 67:5)

For the second time (v. 3) all the peoples are called to shout out in praise of the one true God. The word *all*, occurring four times in our psalm, anticipates the glorious vision in heaven described in Revelation 7:9–10:

After this I looked, and behold, a great multitude that no one could number, from every nation, from all tribes and peoples and languages, standing before the throne and before the Lamb, clothed in white robes, with palm branches in their hands, and crying out with a loud voice, "Salvation belongs to our God who sits on the throne, and to the Lamb! (ESV)

The shining face of God (v. 1) moves "all the peoples" to exult in Him. Betty Stam loved to exult in this God and penned the following as an expression of her heart for the Savior she loved, died for, and sought to make known among the nations.

O Jesus Christ, Thou Son of God and Son of Man,
Thy love no angel understands, nor mortal can!

Thy strength of soul, Thy radiant purity,
Thine understanding heart of sympathy,
The vigor of Thy mind, Thy poetry
Thy heavenly wisdom, Thy simplicity,
Such sweetness and such power in harmony!

Thy perfect oneness with Thy God above;
The agony endured to show Thy love!
Thou who didst rise triumphantly to prove
Thou are the Living God, before whom death
And hell itself must shake and move!

Thou Son of God—
Grant me *Thy face to see*,
Thy voice to hear, *Thy glory share*;
Never apart from Thee,
Ever Thine own to be,
Throughout eternity.[17]

Did you note, "thy glory share"? Did she have in mind His passion and her sharing in it in some sense? Those who knew her believed so. Words like these no doubt are what moved her father to say of his darling daughter following her death, "It almost seemed as though, out of her peaceful, sheltered life, she has prescience of terrible things she would someday encounter for the Lord, and be called to suffer for His dear sake."[18]

God's Goodness Must Be Known among the Nations (*Ps. 67:6–7*)

Initially John Stam's family was not enthusiastic about international missions for their children. After all, we should not overlook the needs at home. Yet John's father, in particular, would be won over by the heart of his son who said, "The Lord knows where he wants me, whether in Holland, in Paterson, or some place in the States, in China, or in India. However, it does look frightfully disproportionate to see so many here in comparison with the few over yonder."[19]

John understood that the goodness of God and his salvation is not limited in scope. God loves to bless His people to "the ends of the earth" (v. 7 ESV), and he desires to do it spiritually and physically, personally and cosmically. The final stanza of Psalm 67 promises a bountiful and fruitful harvest. In lands where people live from day to day and starvation is an ever present danger, an abundant harvest would cause great rejoicing and enthusiastic celebration. It would be the evidence of the gracious blessing of God on his people and a sign to the nations that this God can be trusted, and therefore we should worship him, trust him, and fear him, no matter what.

God Desires to Bless Us (Ps. 67:6)

Verse 6 is stated in the past tense, but it has a forward perspective as does the rest of the psalm. It is a Hebrew way of affirming the certainty of something that will come to pass. With confidence we can believe a harvest will occur, and with confidence we can trust that our God will bless us. The phrase "God, our God," is virtually equivalent in meaning to the covenant name of God, *"Yahweh"* (translated LORD in all caps in most English translations). Those who seek, trust, proclaim, praise, and fear this covenant-keeping God will find him faithful, and they will be blessed by him.

Following his murder, those who sat under John Stam's preaching in the States would say, "Among his special Bible verses were: 'Thou wilt keep in perfect peace whose mind is stayed on Thee,' and; 'The Lord is my helper, I will not fear, what shall man do to me.' Faithfulness was a theme he loved to dwell upon: both in the Christian life and God's own faithfulness to us. How he could sing, 'Great is His Faithfulness.' His life was full of the promises of God."[20]

God Expects Us to Honor Him (Ps. 67:7)

The great missionary Hudson Taylor said, "A little thing is a little thing, but faithfulness in a little thing is a great thing."[21] Verse 7 begins like verse 6 ends: on the theme of God blessing his people, blessings intended to result in the salvation of the nations. God is good to us in sovereign, providential care in order to be savingly gracious to the nations, to "all the ends of the earth" (ESV). He wants all the ends of the earth to know him (v. 2), He wants them to "fear him" (revere him; v. 7). Derek Kidner says, "Let God who brings much out of little and distributes it in love, bring such blessing on us, as to make us, in our turn, the blessing of the world."[22] God indeed performed such a work in John and Betty Stam but not in the way we most likely would have expected.

It is hard to understand why God would see fit to cut short the lives and ministry of such faithful servants as John and Betty Stam. The secret things truly do belong to the Lord (Deut. 29:29). Having married on October 25, 1933, in China, God would grace them with a daughter, Helen Priscilla, born in September 1934. However, the Chinese Communist Civil War was now spreading rapidly into their region, and their attempt to evade marauding bandits was unsuccessful. What follows is a brief account of the final days of their lives.[23]

> Betty was bathing three-month-old Helen when Tsingteh's city magistrate appeared. Communist forces were near, he warned, and urged the Stams to flee. But before the Stams could make their break, the Communists were inside the city. Communist bandits quickly came pounding at their door. John opened it and spoke courteously to the four leaders who entered, asking them if they were hungry. Betty brought them tea and cakes. The courtesy, however, meant nothing. They demanded all the money the Stams had, and John willingly handed it over. John was then bound and led away.
>
> Before long, the bandits reappeared, taking Betty and Helen. That night John was allowed to write a letter to mission authorities, "My wife, baby and myself are today in the hands of the Communists in the city of Tsingteh. Their demand is twenty thousand dollars for our release. The Lord bless and guide you. As for us, may God be glorified, whether by life or by death." The letter was not received until after their murder.
>
> Prisoners in the local jail were released to make room for the Stams. At one point frightened by rifle fire, little Helen began to cry. One of the Communist rebels said, "Let's kill the baby. It is in our way." A bystander asked, "Why kill her? What harm has she

done?" "Are you a Christian?" shouted one of the guards. The man said he was not but that he was one of the prisoners just released. "Will you die for this foreign baby?" they asked. As Betty hugged Helen to her chest, the man was hacked to pieces before all of their eyes.

The next morning their captors led the Stams toward Miaosheo on a twelve mile march. Under guard, the entire Stam's family was taken into a postmaster's shop. "Where are you going?" asked the postmaster, who recognized them from their previous visits to his town. "We do not know where they are going, but we are going to heaven," answered John.

That night the three were held in the house of a wealthy man who had fled. They were carefully guarded by soldiers. John was tied to a post all that cold night, but Betty was allowed enough freedom to tend to the baby. As it turned out, she did more than that.

The next morning the young couple was led through town without the baby. Their hands were tightly bound, and they were stripped of their outer garments as if they were common criminals. John walked barefoot. He had given his socks to Betty. The soldiers jeered and called the town's folk to come see the execution. The terrified people obeyed.

On the way to the execution, a medicine-seller, considered a lukewarm Christian at best, stepped from the crowd and pleaded for the lives of the two foreigners. The Communist bandits angrily ordered him back. The man, however, would not be quiet. His house was searched, a Bible and hymnbook found, and he also was dragged away to be executed as a hated and despised Christian.

John pleaded for the man's life. The bandit's leader sharply ordered him to kneel. As John was speaking softly, the Communist leader swung his sword through the missionary's throat so that his head was severed from his body. Betty did not scream. She quivered and fell bound beside her husband's body. As she knelt there, the same sword ended her life with a single blow.

For two days, local Christians huddled in hiding in the hills around Miaosheo. Among them was a Chinese evangelist named Mr. Lo. Through informants, he learned that the Communists had captured two foreigners. At first he did not realize that it was John and Betty Stam. As soon as government troops entered the valley and it was safe to venture forth, Mr. Lo hurried to town.

An old woman told Pastor Lo that a small baby had been left behind. She pointed in the direction of the house where John and Betty had been chained their last night on earth. Pastor Lo hurried to the site and found room after room trashed by the bandits. Then he heard a muffled cry. Tucked by her mother in a little sleeping bag, Helen was warm and alive, although hungry after her two day fast.

The kindly pastor took the child in his arms and carried her to his wife. With the help of a local Christian family, he wrapped the bodies that still lay upon the hillside and placed them into coffins. To the crowd that gathered he explained that the missionaries had only come to tell them how they might find forgiveness of sin in Jesus Christ. Leaving others to bury the dead, he hurried home. Somehow Helen had to be carried to safety.

Pastor Lo had to find a way to move the children a hundred miles through mountains infested by bandits and Communists. Brave men were found who were willing to help bear the children to safety, but there was no money to pay them for their efforts. Lo had been robbed of everything he had.

But from beyond the grave, Betty had provided. Tucked in Helen's sleeping bag were a change of clothes and some diapers. Pinned between these articles of clothing were two five-dollar bills. It made the difference. Placing the children in rice baskets slung from the two ends of a bamboo pole, the group departed quietly, taking turns carrying the precious cargo over their shoulders. Mrs. Lo was able to find Chinese mothers along the way to nurse Helen.

Eight days after the Stams died in Communist hands, another missionary in a nearby city heard a knock at his door. He opened it and a Chinese woman, stained with travel, entered the house, bearing a bundle in her arms. "This is all we have left," she said brokenly.

Helen Pricilla Stam was three months old when her parents were killed in China, but by God's grace she had survived. She was brought to the United States and was cared for by her maternal grandparents, who had also been missionaries in China, until she was five years old. She then was adopted by her mother's sister and her husband who were missionaries in the Philippines. She grew up in the Philippines and returned to the United States for college, after which she was involved in student work for her denomination.

A small group of Christians took the bodies of John and Betty Stam and buried them on a hillside. Their gravestones read:[24]

John Cornelius Stam, January 18, 1907, "That Christ may be glorified whether by life or death." Philippians 1:20.

Elizabeth Scott Stam, February 22, 1906, "For me to live is Christ and to die is gain." Philippians 1:21.

Daniel Bays would later note, "The courage of the Stams inspired many others to become missionaries."[25]

Conclusion

The brutal murder of John and Betty Stam was met with shock, tears, and grief all around the world. And yet the miraculous preservation of little Helen was an occasion for thanksgiving to God. Our Lord's ways were certainly mysterious in all of this, and yet Betty's parents, with great trust in the providence of God, would say, "Everything about [Helen's] deliverance tells of God's love and power. And we know that if He could bring a tiny, helpless infant, not three months old, through such dangers in perfect safety, He could no less surely have saved the lives of her precious parents, had that been His divine plan for them."[26]

Kenneth, Betty's younger brother would say, "I am a Christian and I can see God's hand behind it all. Instead of throwing us into despondency, it fills us with a greater trust in God, and a greater determination to serve Him with our lives. We do not see the meaning of it all, now, but some day we shall understand. . . . In God's work, the value of a life lived for Him, is measured not by the length, but the quality of service, and by the fulfillment of His purpose for that life. Surely His purposes were fulfilled in Betty and John, and are being fulfilled: so their service was complete."[27]

And Francis, the older brother of Betty and a student at Princeton, would powerfully pray, "May God release to the whole Church new power through this tragedy, and a deeper consecration and more faithful witness to the wonderful cause of Christ, for which true followers all down the ages have been ready and willingly to die."[28]

Finally, from the Congo, John's missionary brother Harry Stam would say, "How sad and yet how glorious! How sad to think of the sin and hatred in the heart of man! And death is still an enemy. But how glorious the welcome that was theirs in heaven, as they met their Lord and Savior face to face! It almost makes one envy them, just a little, to think of the infinite tenderness which He must have said, 'Well done . . . thou has been faithful.'"[29]

A short time before their deaths, John wrote his father informing him of the growing dangers they faced. In the letter he copied some verses that, though written by another, well expressed his and Betty's heart. Would to God they would also express our hearts.

Afraid?
Afraid? Of what?
To feel the spirit's glad release?
To pass from pain to perfect peace,
The strife and strain of life to cease?
Afraid—of that?

Afraid? Of what?
Afraid to see the Savior's face,
To hear His welcome, and to trace
The glory gleam from wounds of grace?
Afraid—of that?

Afraid? Of what?
A flash—a crash—a pierced heart;
Darkness—Light—O Heaven's art?
A wound of His a counterpart!
Afraid?—of that?

Afraid? Of what?
To do by death what life could not—
Baptize with blood a stony plot,
Till souls shall blossom from the spot?
Afraid?—of that?[30]

Oh precious Lord Jesus, be gracious to us and bless us and make your face shine upon us, that your way may be known on the earth, your saving power among all nations! Help us to love you more than we fear man and what he might do to us. Bless us as you blessed John and Betty Stam, if it be your will.

CHAPTER 10

The Vision of the Exalted Lamb Realized in the Life of Missionary James Fraser among the Lisu People of China

Revelation 5:8–10

 While James Fraser (1886–1938) was still a student at London University, he was given a booklet entitled *Do Not Say*, in which he read these indicting words:

A command has been given: "Go ye into all the world and preach the Gospel to every creature." It has not been obeyed. More than half the people in the world have never yet heard the Gospel. What are we to say to this? Surely it concerns us Christians very seriously. For we are the people who are responsible. . . . If our Master returned today to find millions of people un-evangelised, and looked as of course He would look, to us for an explanation, I cannot imagine what explanation we should have to give. . . . Of one thing I am certain—that most of the excuses we are accustomed to make with such good conscience now, we should be wholly ashamed of then.[1]

These words, written by a missionary in China, compelled Fraser, an accomplished concert pianist and honor student in engineering, to leave England and run to China where he gave the rest of his life that the Lisu people might exalt the Lamb, the Lord Jesus, who redeemed us to God by his blood.

Revelation 7:9–10 gives us an incredible vision of heaven. There we read, "After these things I looked, and behold, a great multitude which no one could number, of all nations, tribes, peoples, and tongues, standing before the throne and before the Lamb, clothed with white robes, with palm branches in their hands, and crying out with a loud voice, saying, "Salvation *belongs* to our God who sits on the throne, and to the Lamb!" (NKJV). However, the foundation for this remarkable celebration and worship of those who have "washed their robes and made them white in the blood of the lamb" (Rev. 7:15) is actually found in Revelation 5. God uses men like James Fraser to see to it that every tribe and tongue and people and nation will be there to worship the exalted Lamb.

After reading the little booklet *Do Not Say*, James Fraser could not escape the words of conviction it contained. The year was 1906. He was twenty years old. The need of the nations was too great. The realities of eternity were too overwhelming. Once when considering the lostness of the people God sent him to reach, he said,

The whole plain . . . is without the light of the Gospel.
I believe God would be glorified by even one witness
to His name amid the perishing thousands. It does
seem a terrible thing that so few are offering for the
mission field. I can't help feeling that there is something wrong somewhere. Surely God must be wanting
His people to go forward. Does not the Master's last
command still hold good?[2]

This passion sent James Fraser to China for thirty years of
faithful, gospel ministry for King Jesus. It was only after being
rejected twice by the Mission Board that Fraser was finally
sent out. As a matter of fact on his third attempt, perhaps
anticipating another letter of rejection, he stated, "Well I am
going there anyway because I know I've been sent by God."[3]
This passion would sustain him through kidnapping, mul-
tiple robberies, leg ulcers, lice, rats, malaria, total exhaustion,
and mental and spiritual depression that nearly drove him to
suicide. As his daughter Eileen Crossman would write in her
biography about her father,

He was assailed by deep and treacherous doubts. Yea,
hath God said? The question came to him again and
again, as clearly as it came at the dawn of time. Your
prayers are not being answered, are they? No one wants
to hear your message. The few who first believed have
gone back, haven't they? You see, it doesn't work. You
should never have stayed in this area on such a fool's
errand. You've been in China five years and there's
not much to show for it, is there? You thought you
were called to be a missionary. It was pure imagina-
tion. You'd better leave it all, go back and admit it
was a big mistake. Day after day and night after night

he wrestled with doubt and suicidal despair. Suicidal? Not once, but several times he stared over the dark ravine into the abyss. Why not end it all? The powers of darkness had him isolated; if they could get him now they could put an end to the work.[4]

Yet, as Revelation 12:11 so wonderfully says, he overcame the evil one by the blood of the Lamb and the word of his testimony, and he did not love his life in the face of death. He persevered and the Lamb honored his faithfulness. What are the lessons God would have us learn from this text so faithfully displayed in the life of one of his superlative servants among the nations? I would like to highlight three.

The Prayers of the Saints Contribute to the Redeeming of the Nations (*Rev. 5:8*)

Revelation 5:8 is filled with drama. The Lamb who alone is worthy to approach the throne of God has stepped forward (v. 7) and taken the scroll, which when opened (6:1), unveils the remainder of the book of Revelation (chapters 6–22). As he takes the scroll from the hand of his Father who sits on heaven's throne (4:1), worship explodes in heaven! First, the four living creatures, angelic beings, fall down in worship. Joining them are the twenty-four elders, representing the redeemed of all the ages. Dropping to their knees and placing their faces on the floor, they prepare to sing the new song of redemption found in the next verse. They hold in one hand a harp, an instrument of praise, and in the other they hold bowls full of sweet smelling incense that John tells us "are the prayers of the saints." Make sure you don't miss this.

Sometimes when we pray, we wonder if God hears. We wonder if our prayers ever escape the ceiling just above our heads. James Fraser certainly struggled with this spiritual challenge, "I suppose we have most of us had such experiences. We have prayed and prayed and prayed and no answer has come. The heavens above us have been as brass. Yes, blessed brass, if it has taught us to sink a little more of this ever-present self of ours into the Cross of Christ."[5] Fraser believed that prayer drives us down in humility as our prayers go up before the throne of God. And "Yes, He hears them," and they are being collected in heaven as a pleasant aroma of worship. From the context it would appear that prayers for the salvation of the nations are particularly the kind of prayers that please our God.

It would not be a stretch to describe James Fraser as a "prayer missionary." Born in England in 1886, he was one of six children from a broken home. He would not marry his wife Roxie until the age of forty-three and then die at age fifty-two. For years his godly mother prayed that at least one of her children would become a missionary. God heard and answered that prayer! In fact, his mother wrote, "I could not pour out the ointment on [Jesus] blessed feet as Mary did, but I gave Him my boy."[6] James would gladly say his missionary call was the result of his mother's prayers. God hears the prayers of godly mothers and fathers for their children.

In fact, prayer engulfed his missionary ministry both at home in England and on the field in China. Speaking of his burden for the lost, Fraser would write, "I was very much led out in prayer for these people, right from the beginning. Something seemed to draw me to them, and the desire of my heart grew until it became a burden that God would give us hundreds of converts among the Lisu of our western district."[7]

In a letter to a friend requesting prayer partners, Fraser said, "Solid, lasting missionary work is done on our knees. What I covet more than anything else is earnest, believing prayer, and I write to ask you to continue to put up much prayer for me and the work here."[8] Elsewhere, he would write, "I will not labor the point. You will see from what I am saying that I am not asking you just to give us 'help' in prayer as a sort of sideline, but I am trying to roll the main responsibility of the prayer warfare on you. I want you to take the burden of these people upon your shoulders. I want you to wrestle with God for them."[9] The impact of prayer in Fraser's ministry can be seen in these words: "If I am sure of anything it is that your prayers have made a very real difference to my life and service."[10]

In reference to the necessity and power of prayer for all believers, whether on the mission field or not, Fraser wrote:

> I am feeling more and more that it is, after all, just the prayers of God's people that call down blessing upon the work, whether they are directly engaged in it or not. Paul may plant and Apollos water, but it is God who gives the increase; and this increase can be brought down from heaven by believing prayer. . . . We are, as it were, God's agents—used by him to do his work, not ours. We do our part, and then can only look to him, with others, for his blessing. If this is so, then Christians at home can do as much for foreign missions as those actually on the field. I believe it will only be known on the last day how much has been accomplished in missionary work by the prayers of earnest believers at home. And this, surely, is the heart of the problem.[11]

Fraser realized, in the words of John Piper, "that prayer is meant by God to be a wartime walkie-talkie, not a domestic intercom . . . not for the enhancement of our comforts but for the advancement of Christ's kingdom."[12] Ephesians 6:18–20 sees prayers as a weapon in spiritual warfare to be used for the advancing of God's kingdom through the gospel. Fraser described this kind of spiritual warfare when he wrote:

> One of the temptations in the spirit-warfare is when your body begins to flag, to say, "I must give up," instead of casting yourself upon "God that raised the dead" and can quicken the mortal body to endure and triumph in and through all things. Oh how we need STRENGTH, for often we can hardly hold our ground! (Eph 6:10). In every battle there are crucial spots. Get near and stay near to your Divine Chief until He turns and points them out. And at those points face and force the fight. And though the conflict be keen, though defeat seems certain, though the battle should continue for hours, for days, for months, even for years, yet hold on, HOLD ON; for to such Jer 1:19 is written: "They shall fight against thee but they shall not prevail against thee, for I am with thee to deliver thee." *The aim of Satanic power is to cut off communication with God.* To accomplish this aim he deludes the soul with a sense of defeat, covers him with a thick cloud of darkness, depresses and oppresses the spirit, which in turn hinders prayer and leads to unbelief—thus destroying all power (instead of seeing Heb 11:1).[13]

The following excerpts from Fraser's journal reveal how he used the prayer on the front lines of ministry:

> Seem distinctly led (he wrote) to fight against "principalities and powers" for Middle Village. Have faith for the conversion of that place, and pray as a kind of bugle-call for the hosts of heaven to come down and

fight for me against the powers of darkness holding these two old men who are hindering their villages and perhaps three others from turning to Christ. *Have a good time of fighting prayer, then sleep in much peace of mind.*[14]

The whole cause of my defeat these two days is weakness of spirit. Under these conditions, any test you take fails to work. *The spirit must be continually maintained in strength by unceasing prayer, especially against the powers of darkness. All I have learned of other aspects of the victory-life is useless without this.*[15]

This kind of prayer-life kept him going when seriously ill, kidnapped, robbed, depressed, nearly drowning in a monsoon mudslide, which did take the life of the horse he was riding, and working day after day among a demon-worshipping people seeing little or no results. A prayer-life of faith in the God who answers prayer could keep him in the fight and lead him to write this in his journal after a day's travel in a fierce blizzard:

You arrive at the end of the day cold, hungry and tired, not to find a nice clean room waiting for you, a warm bath, a warm fire, a smile of welcome and a nice meal! No, you, splash along the slushy street from dismal inn to dismal inn . . . and you get suspicious stares. Finally you practically force your way into an inn. It is pitch dark; the floor is a mess; there is no furniture but a mud platform, no light, no warmth. . . . You and your muleteer make a meal of plain boiled rice. But next morning you get out again into your blue skies and snow mountains and forget all your previous night's troubles.[16]

In the life of James Fraser, we learn that the prayers of the saints contribute to the redeeming of the nations. God hears those prayers. They are not wasted.

The Blood of Christ Has Purchased the Salvation of the Nations (*Rev. 5:9*)

Verse 9 contains one of the great songs of redemption. It is called a "new" song, meaning a new *kind* of song made possible by the slaughtered Lamb now standing strong as seen in verse 6. He and he alone is *worthy* (a word used four times in chapter 5 [vv. 2, 4, 9, 12]) to take the scroll from God the Father who sits upon the throne. Why? Four reasons are given.

1. You were slain (v. 9).
2. You redeemed us to God by your blood (v. 9).
3. You have made us kings and priests to our God (v. 10).
4. Those you have redeemed will reign with you on the earth (v. 10).

Redeemed by his blood! Not a happy thought among liberal theologians. It is nothing more than foolishness to those who are perishing. A dead Galilean Jew nailed to a cross; bleeding all over the place, is the means whereby God redeems the nations? Are you kidding me? Are you serious? That is the view of Delores Williams of Union Theological Seminary in New York: "I don't think we need a theory of atonement at all. I don't think we need folks hanging on crosses and blood dripping and weird stuff."[17] Virginia Mollenkott says the death of Jesus was nothing less than the ultimate in child abuse. God is an abusive parent and Jesus an obedient and abused child. Rt. Rev. Jeffrey John of the Church of England calls a bloody atonement "repulsive" and "insane." In fact, listen to his exact words for just a moment:

The explanation I was given went something like this. God was very angry with us for our sins, and because he is a just God, our sin had to be punished. But instead of punishing us he sent his Son, Jesus, as a substitute to suffer and die in our place. The blood of Jesus paid the price of our sins, and because of him God stopped being angry with us. In other words, Jesus took the rap, and we got forgiven, provided we said we believed in him. Well, I don't know about you, but even at the age of ten I thought this explanation was *pretty repulsive* as well as *nonsensical*. What sort of God was this, getting so angry with the world and the people he created, and then, to *calm himself down*, demanding the blood of his own Son? And anyway, why should God forgive us through punishing somebody else? It was worse than illogical, it was *insane*. It made God sound like a *psychopath*. If any human being behaved like that we'd say they were a *monster*. Well I haven't changed my mind since. That explanation of the cross doesn't work, though sadly it's one that's still all too often preached. It just doesn't make sense to talk about a nice Jesus down here, placating the wrath of a nasty, angry Father God in heaven.[18]

Tragically a growing number of so-called evangelicals could be added to these three, but praise God, James Fraser would not be one of them. Here are his thoughts about his Lord's cross.

Gaining victory in spiritual warfare: "I read [*The Overcomer*] over and over. . . . What it showed me was the deliverance from the power of the evil one comes through definite resistance on the grounds of the cross."[19]

Preaching the Gospel: I first went through the Acts of the Apostles and some other passages, comparing them with a view to finding out the actual Gospel we are bidden to preach. . . . The result was very instructive to me. I had never imagined the Gospel was so simple. Why, Peter and Paul both preached the Gospel in words which would not take one minute to say! And I found out that there are just four things which seem to be essential in preaching the Gospel.

1. The crucifixion of Jesus Christ.
2. The resurrection of Jesus Christ—most important of all. The Gospel was never preached without this being brought in.
3. Exhortation to hearers to repent of their sins.
4. Promise to all who believe on Jesus Christ that they will receive remission of their sins.

Beyond these four points others are mentioned occasionally, but they are not many. . . . In teaching Christians, it is quite another matter. To them we are to declare "the whole counsel of God," as far as they can receive it. But the Gospel as preached to the unsaved is as simple as it could be. I should not care to take the responsibility of preaching "another Gospel."[20]

The power of the cross: The ground of the cross was what brought me light. For I found that it worked. I felt like a man perishing of thirst, to whom some beautiful, clear cold water had begun to flow.[21]

I have no confidence in anything but the Gospel of Calvary to uplift these needy people.[22]

Quite conscience of Mother's prayers I am sure she is praying for me. Splendid time of prayer alone in my room enabled to get to the cross and remain there. Have peace and rest of spirit.[23]

Very definitely and decidedly take my stand on 1 John 1:7—Jesus Christ my Cleanser from all sin. Full of peace and blessing all the rest of the day.[24]

The Gospel of a broken heart begins the ministry of bleeding hearts. As soon as we cease to bleed we cease to bless. We must bleed if we would be ministers of the Saving Blood.[25]

The cross may be foolishness to the world, but it is the power of God to salvation according to the Scriptures. And so it was in the life of James Fraser. He could say with the apostle Paul, "But far be it from me to boast except in the cross of our Lord Jesus Christ, by which the world has been crucified to me, and I to the world." We too can boast in the cross because on it Christ was slain, and by his blood he purchased the salvation of the nations.

The Redeemed Serve as a Kingdom of Priests in Reaching the Nations (*Rev. 5:10*)

The exalted Lamb redeemed us to reign with Him. He has "made us kings" or "a kingdom." As Romans 8:16–17 teaches, "The Spirit Himself bears witness with our spirit that we are children of God, and if children, then heirs—heirs of God and joint heirs with Christ, if indeed we suffer with Him, that we may also be glorified together" (NKJV).

The exalted Lamb redeemed us to serve Him. We are each and every one of us "priests to our God." Priests represent God to man among the nations, having come from his presence saved and sanctified by precious blood, the blood of the exalted Lamb. James Fraser was a marvelous priest of God to man. Without question the keys to his walk with God were a life immersed in prayer, fasting and other spiritual disciplines. Just one month before his untimely death at the age of fifty-two he wrote, "I often think that it is the very, very few who are prepared, by rigorous self-discipline (not a very popular thing nowadays), for a lifetime of great usefulness."[26]

On one occasion James found a man dying on the side of the road apparently ignored by others. He picked him up and carried him on his back for six miles to get him help. It was this sacrificial act of service that God would use to bring a Burmese man named Chang to Christ.[27] Some called him strange and eccentric! I call him Christlike!

What drove James Fraser to live as such a Christlike servant of God in reaching the nations? His own words provide the best answer:

> It is all IF and WHEN, I believe the devil is fond of those conjunctions. . . . The plain truth is that the Scriptures never teach us to wait for opportunities of service, but to serve in just the things that lie next to our hands. . . . The Lord bids us work, watch and pray; but Satan suggests, wait until a good opportunity for working, watching and praying presents itself— and needless to say, this opportunity is always in the future. . . . Since the things that lie in our immediate path have been ordered of God, who shall say that one kind of work is more important and sacred than another? I believe it is no more necessary to be faithful

(one says it reverently) in preaching the Gospel than in washing up dishes. It is not for us, in any case, to choose our work. And if God has chosen it for us, hadn't we better go straight ahead and do it, without waiting for anything greater, better or "nobler"?[28]

This "state of mind" and heart kept him going. The following record from his journal puts this state of mind on display. On a particular Sunday, **January 16**, "Not a single one to Service in the morning." **January 18**, "Abraham was called out by God and went in blind faith; when he got to the land of promise, he found nothing but a famine—much like me with the Lisu, these two years." **February 3**, "Depressed after defeat this morning, from which no real recovery all day. **February 4**, "No meal until 2 p.m. Thoroughly depressed about the state of work in Tantsah. No one to count upon in matters demanding an earnest spirit. The evil one seems to have the upper hand in me today."[29]

But James Fraser pressed on in prayer and in service. **February 5**, "Yesterday's attack of depression and defeat almost got over, but not quite. Such times are not easy to recover from, I find. . . . The majority of Christians have gone in for whisky-drinking. . . . The outlook here in Tantsah at present seems less hopeful than at any time since I first set foot in the place. I am not, however, taking the black, despondent view I took yesterday . . . the opposition will not be overcome by reasoning or by pleading, but by (chiefly) steady, persistent prayer. The men need not be dealt with (it is a heart-breaking job, trying to deal with a Lisu possessed by a spirit of fear) but the powers of darkness need to be fought. I am now setting my face like a flint: if the work seems to fain, then *pray*; if services etc., fall flat, then *pray still more*; if months slip by with little or no result, then *pray still more and get others to* *help you.* **Sunday, February 6**, B. and Va announce they will become Christians, if their parents will allow them. . . . Four young men say they will follow Christ, whatever happens. . . . **Tuesday, February 8**, Mo La P turns Christian in the morning. Gu Va and T, all at his house. . . . Full of joy and praise."[30]

Service as a kingdom of priests in the drama of redemption is not always easy. It can be discouraging and even depressing, as Fraser's experience has shown. But it will be fruitful and rewarding if we will persevere and stay at it. It may be five plus years before we see the fruit of our labor. Like Carey and Judson, it may be seven! But rest assured, the Father hears the prayers of his children, and he sees their labor of love for the Exalted Lamb and the souls of the nations. To participate in this wonderful drama of redemption entails a wonderful certainty: I will not look back at the end of my days and lament, "I lived a wasted life!"

Conclusion

James Fraser's death came suddenly and unexpectedly. Neither his family nor the Lisu people were prepared for the home going of this great man of God. His daughter records his death with these words:

> "You know, Roxie," James said one day up in the hills, "Even when I've gone, I don't think my work in Yunnan will be finished." She was startled a few days later when he said, "Mr. Payne is passing through in two weeks' time. I have some money here for him. If anything happens to me, you'll know where it is." "But I don't understand" [she said]—[He responded] "I just thought I'd let you know." He talked a lot these days about the children's future and about the baby expected [their third] before the end of the year. It

was September already: the event was not too far off. On Wednesday, September 21, James had a headache. He finished answering some important letters and then played the little organ for a while before going to bed. By the next morning his headache was severe. He sent runners at once to get someone to be with Roxie. James had gone down with malignant cerebral malaria. There was no appropriate medicine in Paoshan. It was not long before he lost consciousness, and for two days the fever intensified; by Saturday evening he was strangely quiet. It was a long night for Roxie: James in and out of delirium, the Chinese doctor and nurses hurrying up and down the stairs, the child crying in the darkness. *When the sun rose on September 25, 1938, James had gone.* It was a shock to his colleagues. He was only 52 and seemed strong and healthy: they found the news hard to believe. But for Roxie the whole world was reeling. Isobel Kuhn wrote to her three days later: "The very thought of you makes my hand tremble so and the tears come so that I do not know how I can write. The Lisu have just walked in with their unbelievable message. . . . Times like this are when we just have to bare our face to the tempest and go on without seeing clearly, without understanding, without anything but naked faith.[31]

How do we summarize a man that Stuart Simpson, an actor who portrayed James Fraser in the short documentary *Breakthrough*, called "one of the most successful Christian missionaries in East Asia in modern times!", a man of whom his biographer said, "The young man handed over not the latch key but the master key of his whole being"?[32]

It would be five plus years before what is called "the break-through" would occur, but within four months six hundred Lisu representing 129 families turned to Christ. Revival broke out spreading from mountain village to mountain village. By 1918, ten years into the work, sixty thousand believers had been baptized. What an awesome God we serve! Today there are an estimated 300,000 Lisu Christians in Western China and thousands more in Myanmar and Thailand.

Before his death James Fraser devised the first written script for the Lisu people. It was officially recognized by the Chinese government in 1992. He would lead the way in trans-lating the New Testament into Lisu. His humility, servant spirit, and dependence on God made him so useful to the Exalted Lamb. Before they married, Roxie, his bride-to-be said, "Never once did he tell me the way he had been used among the Lisu."[33] Friend Isobel Kuhn, describing the testi-mony of Fraser following his sudden and untimely death at fifty-two from cerebral malaria in 1938 said: "He never disap-pointed us in the sharing. . . . He was our missionary ideal, a continual rebuke, challenge and stimulus to maintain at any cost the apostolic methods of missionary work. His brilliant gifts, united with unfailing humility and a sympathy mother-like in tenderness and thoughtfulness, made him our refuge at all times of perplexity and need."[34]

At the beginning of the book *Mountain Rain*, a biography of James Fraser, the story is told of how James was able on one occasion to outrun for hours a Kachin tribesman intent on murdering him. James was comforted by the truth, as was Lottie Moon and Jim Elliott, "A Christian is immortal till his work is done."[35] Then toward the end of the book, following her father's death, Eileen tells us this: "A man came to visit [my mother] before she sailed. He was a Kachin Christian and badly wanted to meet her. Years before, he said, he had run many miles to kill James Fraser, but James out ran him. Sometime later he heard the message of Jesus Christ; he had believed and became his disciple."[36]

To hear of such a wonderful conversion would not have surprised James Fraser after thirty years of service in China. He had come to well understand who we are and what we do, and who God is and how he works! Frasier had discovered:

> On the human side, evangelistic work on the mission field is like a man going about in a dark, damp valley with a lighted match in his hand, seeking to ignite anything ignitable. But things are damp through and through and will not burn, however much he tries. In other cases, God's wind and sunshine have prepared beforehand. The valley is dry in places, and when the lighted match is applied—here a shrub, there a tree, here a few sticks, there a heap of leaves take fire and give light and warmth *long after the kindling match and its bearer have passed on*. And this is what God wants to see, and what he will inquire of us: *little patches of fire burning all over the world*.[37]

Brothers and sisters, we are to light those "little patches of fire around the world," knowing we are indeed immortal till our work is done. The Exalted Lamb guarantees it!

Notes

Chapter 1

1. Timothy George, *Faithful Witness: The Life and Mission of William Carey* (Downers Grove: IVP, 1992), 93.

2. Ibid., 53.

3. Ibid., 32.

4. William Carey, *An Enquiry into the Obligations of Christians to Use Means for the Conversion of the Heathens* (Dallas: Criswell Publication, 1988).

5. Ibid., 4.

6. Ibid., 56.

7. George, *Faithful Witness*, xii.

8. John Piper, "Worship the Risen Christ," *desiringgod.org*, April 3, 1983, http://www.desiringgod.org/resource-library/sermons/worship-the-risen-christ, accessed August 24, 2011.

9. Quoted in George, *Faithful Witnesses*, 39.

10. Ibid., 39.

11. Ibid., 45.

12. John Piper, "The Lofty Claim, the Last Command, the Loving Comfort," *desiringgod.org*, November 1, 1998, http://www.desiringgod.org/resource-library/sermons/the-lofty-claim-the-last-command-the-loving-comfort, accessed August 24, 2011.

13. R. T. France, *Matthew.* NICNT (Grand Rapids: Eerdmans, 2007), 1114.

14. William Carey, *The Journal and Selected Letters of William Carey*, ed. Terry G. Carter (Macon, GA: Smyth & Helwys, 2000), 21.

15. Carey, 65.

16. James M. Boice, *The Gospel of Matthew* (Grand Rapids: Baker, 2006), 649.

17. Quoted in George, *Faithful Witness*, 94.

18. Ibid., 154.

19. Ibid., 25.

20. Carter, 39.

21. G. Campbell Morgan, *The Gospel According to Matthew* (New York: Fleming H. Revell, 1929), 320–21.

22. Carey, 55–56.

23. George, 155.

24. Ibid., 168.

Chapter 2

1. Significant biographical information for this sermon came from Courtney Anderson, *To the Golden Shore: The Life of Adoniram Judson* (Boston: Brown, Little, and Company, 1956; reprint, Valley Forge, PA: Judson, 1987).

2. Eugene Myers Harrison, *Giants of the Missionary Trail: The Life Stories of Eight Men Who Defied Death and Demons* (Chicago, IL: Scripture Press, 1954), available online at http://www.wholesome-words.org/missions/giants/biojudson2.html.

3. Fred Barlow, *Profiles in Evangelism: Biographical Sketches of World-Renowned Soul Winners* (Murfreesboro, TN: Sword of the Lord, 1976), 103.

4. Anderson, 46.

5. Barlow, 104.

6. Anderson, 44.

7. Barlow, 104.

8. Ibid.

9. Anderson, 59.

10. Edward Judson, *The Life of Adoniram Judson* (New York: A. D. F. Randolph, 1883), 20.

11. Ibid., 20–21.

12. Anderson, 221.

13. Ibid., 334.

14. Ibid., 349.

15. Harrison, *Giants of the Missionary Trail*.

16. Anderson, 365.

17. Ibid., 370.

18. Ibid., 390.

19. Ibid., 391.

20. Harrison, *Giants of the Missionary Trail*.

21. Ibid.

22. Anderson, 399.

Chapter 3

1. Significant biographical information for this sermon came from Jesse C. Fletcher, *Bill Wallace of China* (Nashville: B&H, 1996).

2. Ibid., 16.

3. Ibid., 17.

4. Ibid., 7.

5. Ibid., 24.

6. Ibid., 72.

7. Dan Graves, "Bill Wallace Arrested in Early Morning Raid," http://www.christianity.com/ChurchHistory/11630801, accessed December 1, 2011.

8. Fletcher., 53.

9. Ibid., 137–38.

10. Ibid., 95.

11. Ibid., 89.

12. Ibid., 177.

13. Ibid.

14. Ibid., 129.

15. Ibid., 69.

16. Ibid., 98.

17. Ibid,, 157.

18. Ibid., 113.

19. John Piper, "Jesus Christ: Alive and with Us to the End," *desiringgod.org*, April 23, 2000, http://www.desiringgod.org/resource-library/sermons/jesus-christ-alive-and-with-us-to-the-end, accessed August 24, 2011.

20. Fletcher, 202.

21. Fletcher, 203–8.

22. Ibid., 215.

23. Ibid.

24. The motion picture is also entitled *Bill Wallace of China*. It was originally released in 1967.

25. Visit their Web site at http://www.wmbc.net.

26. Ibid., 252–53.

Chapter 4

1. Significant biographical material for this sermon came from Catherine B. Allen, *The New Lottie Moon Story*, 2nd ed. (Birmingham, AL: Woman's Missionary Union); and Keith Harper, ed., *Send the Light: Lottie Moon's Letters and Other Writings* (Macon, GA: Mercer University Press, 2002).

2. Allen, 11.

3. Ibid., 48.

4. Ibid.

5. Harper, 160–61.

6. Ibid., 224.

7. Allen., 184.

8. Ibid., 39.

9. Ibid., 69.

10. Harper, 89.

11. Quote taken from John Allen Moore, "Lottie's Biography Part 2: The Offering Begins," http://www.imb.org/main/give/page.asp?Story ID=5563&LanguageID=1709, accessed December 1, 2011.

12. Harper., 7.

13. Ibid., 80.

14. Ibid., 17.

15. Ibid., 32.

16. Ibid., 78.

17. Ibid., 83.

18. Quote taken from John Allen Moore, "Lottie's Biography Part 2: The Offering Begins," http://www.imb.org/main/give/page.asp?Story ID=5563&LanguageID=1709, accessed December 1, 2011.

19. Harper, 136.

20. Ibid., 184.

21. Ibid., 225–26.

22. Ibid., 239–40.

23. Ibid., 78–83.

24. Ibid., 33.

25. Allen, 139.

26. Ibid., 172.

27. Ibid., 160.

28. Ibid., 294.

29. Ibid., 160.

30. Ibid.

31. Harper, 256.

32. Ibid., 216.

33. Ibid., 292.

34. Harper, 89.

35. Allen., 287.

36. Ibid., 289.

37. Ibid., 447.

38. Regina D. Sullivan, *Lottie Moon* (Baton Rouge, LA: LSU Press, 2011), 150–54.

39. Allen, 288.

40. Ibid., 289.

41. Ibid., 293.

42. Ibid., 139.

Chapter 5

1. Significant biographical information for this sermon came from Elisabeth Elliot, *Shadow of the Almighty: The Life and Testament of Jim Elliot* (San Francisco: Harper & Row, 1989) and *The Journals of Jim Elliot* (Grand Rapids: Revell, 2002).

2. James M. Boice, *Psalms: An Expositional Commentary*, vol. 2 (Grand Rapids: Baker, 2005), 782.

3. Elliot, *Shadow of the Almighty*, 79.

4. Ibid., 90.

5. Ibid., 90–91.

6. Ibid., 132.

7. Elliot, *The Journals of Jim Elliot*, 402.

8. Ibid., 9.

9. Ibid., 11.

10. Ibid., 247.

11. Ibid., 73.

12. Ibid., 97.

13. Ibid.

14. Ibid.

15. Warren Wiersbe, *The Bible Exposition Commentary* (Wheaton: Victor Books, 1989), 264.

16. *The Journals of Jim Elliot.*, 98.

17. Ibid., 84.

18. Ibid.

19. Ibid. 454.

20. John Piper, *Desiring God* (Colorado Springs: Multnomah, 2011), 10.

21. Elliot, *Shadow of the Almighty*, 81.

22. Quote taken from the motion picture *Beyond the Gates of Splendor.*

23. "Go Ye and Preach the Gospel," *Life Magazine*, January 30, 1956, 10–19.

24. Elliot, *Shadow of the Almighty*, 46.

25. Ibid., 60.

26. Ibid., 244.

27. Elliot, *The Journals of Jim Elliot*, 173–74.

28. Ibid., 174.

29. "Go Ye and Preach the Gospel," 10.

30. Elliot, *Shadow of the Almighty*, 196.

Chapter 6

1. Rev. E. K. Love, *History of the First African Baptist Church* (Savannah, GA: The Morning News Print, 1888), 34.

2. Leroy Fitts, *A History of Black Baptists* (Nashville: Broadman Press, 1985), 109.

3. John MacArthur, *Galatians* (Chicago: Moody, 1987), 200.

4. Edmund Clowney, *Preaching Christ in All of Scripture* (Wheaton: Crossway, 2003), 55.

5. Edward Holmes Jr., "George Liele: Negro Slavery's Prophet of Deliverance," in *Baptist History & Heritage* (August 1965): 25.

6. I have maintained a consistent spelling of the name throughout all references.

7. Quoted in Holmes, 27.

8. Ibid., 28.

9. Eric Hartman, "God Made Men. Men Made Slaves," Semper Reformanda, entry posted February 7, 2008, http://gunny93.blogspot.com/2008/02/god-made-men-men-made-slaves.html, accessed October 7, 2010.

10. Holmes, 31.

11. Charles Spurgeon, "Three Crosses" in *Metropolitan Tabernacle Pulpit*, vol. 24 (Pasadena, TX: Pilgrim Publications, 1972), 674.

12. John Gillies, *Memoirs of George Whitefield* (Middletown: Hunt & Noyes, 1837), 548.

13. Charles Spurgeon, "Grand Glorying" in *Metropolitan Tabernacle Pulpit*, vol. 61 (Pasadena, TX: Pilgrim Publications, 1980), 141.

14. Holmes, 30.

15. Ibid.

16. Holmes, 30.

17. Ibid., 30–31.

18. Ibid., 33.

19. Ibid., 34.

20. Ibid.

21. Ibid.

22. Clarence M. Wagner, *Profiles of Black Georgia Baptists* (Gainesville, GA: Wagner, 1980), 4.

23. Timothy George, *Galatians* (Nashville: B&H, 1994), 439.

24. D. A. Carson, *The Cross and Christian Ministry* (Grand Rapids: Baker, 2004), 9.

25. Hughes Oliphant Old, *The Reading and Preaching of the Scriptures in the Worship of the Christian Church: The Modern Age* (Grand Rapids: Eerdmans, 2007), 585–86.

26. Hartman, 2.

27. David Benedict, *General History of the Baptist Denomination in America and Other Parts of the World* (London: Lincoln & Edmans, 1813), 196.

28. Ibid., 203.

29. C. J. Mahaney, *Living the Cross-Centered Life* (Sisters, OR: Multnomah, 2006), 18.

30. Ibid., 38.

31. George, 442.

32. Jonathan Edwards, *The Salvation of Souls* (Wheaton: Crossway, 2003), 170.

33. Holmes, 32.

34. Benedict, 199.

35. Ibid., 200.

36. Ibid., 201.

37. Love, 37.

38. Holmes, 36.

Chapter 7

1. John Thornburry, *David Brainerd: Pioneer Missionary to the American Indians* (Darlington, England: Evangelical Press, 1996), 298.

2. David Brainerd, *The Life & Diary of David Brainerd* (Grand Rapids: Bakers, 1949), 69–70.

3. See also 1 Timothy 2:7 for these same three assignments.

4. Brainerd, 142.

5. Ibid., 133, 381.

6. Ibid., 133.

7. Ibid., 132.

8. The following excerpts are taken from Brainerd, 166–71.

9. Ibid., 171.

10. Fred Barlow, *Profiles in Evangelism* (Murfreesboro, TN: Sword of the Lord, 1976), 33.

11. Ibid., 33–34.

12. Brainerd, 124.

13. Brainerd, 167.

14. Ibid., 174.

15. Ibid., 203–4.

16. Ibid., 277.

17. Jonathan Edwards, *The Works of Jonathan Edwards*, vol 1. (Peabody, MA: Hendrickson, 1998), lxii–lxiii.

18. cf. 2 Timothy 1:18; the final judgment when Christ returns.

19. Brainerd, 374.

20. The following are taken from Brainerd, 375–76.

21. Brainerd, 336.

22. J. M. Sherwood, *Memoirs of Rev. David Brainerd Missionary to the Indians of North America* (New York: Funk & Wagnalls), xxx.

23. Quoted from F. W. Boreham, *A Casket of Cameos; More Texts That Made History* (New York: Abingdon, 1924), 21.

24. Ibid., 21.

Chapter 8

1. Eric Liddell, *The Disciplines of the Christian Life* (London: SCPK, 2009), 50–51.

2. Dave McCasland, *Eric Liddell: Pure Gold* (Grand Rapids: Discovery House Publishers, 2004), 19.

3. John W. Keddie, *Running the Race* (Darlington, England: Evangelical Press, 2007), 207.

4. Ibid., 163.

5. Ibid.

6. McCasland, 74.

7. McCasland, *Pure Gold*, 71.

8. Liddell, 38.

9. Ibid., 27.

10. Ibid., 32.

11. Ibid., 65.

12. Ibid., 71.

13. Ibid., 73.

14. Ibid., 122.

15. Ibid., 103.

16. Ibid., 116–17.

17. Ibid.

18. Ibid., 77.

19. Ibid., 121.

20. Ibid., 137.

21. Ibid., 72.

22. Ibid., 74.

23. Ibid., 39.

24. Ibid., 36-37.

25. Ibid., 56–58.

26. Ibid., 13–15.

27. Keddie, 193.

28. Quote seen online at http://www.ericliddell.org/eric-liddell/eric-liddell-quotations.php.

29. Keddie, *Running the Race*, 187.

30. Ibid., 189.

31. Ibid., 195.

32. Ibid., 206.

33. McCasland, *Pure Gold*, 285.

34. Ibid., 290.

35. Liddell, 125.

Chapter 9

1. Mrs. Howard Taylor, *To Die Is Gain: The Triumph of John and Betty Stam*. (Denton, TX: Westminster Resources, 2004), 55.

2. Ibid., quote taken from the back cover.

3. Carl Stam, "John & Betty Stam," *CarlStam.org*, http://www.carlstam.org/familyheritage/jbstam.html, accessed August 24, 2011.

4. Taylor, *To Die Is Gain*, 47.

5. Ibid., 5.

6. Ibid.

7. Ibid,, 17.

8. Ibid,, 26.

9. Ibid., 48–49.

10. Ibid., 93.

11. Ibid., 99.

12. Ibid., 98–99.

13. Ibid., 54–56.

14. John Piper, "Let All the Nations Praise Thee," *desiringgod.org*, November 9, 1986, http://www.desiringgod.org/resource-library/sermons/let-all-the-peoples-praise-thee, accessed August 24, 2011.

15. Taylor, *To Die Is Gain*, 35.

16. Ibid.

17. Ibid., 36, italics are mine.

18. Ibid., 39.

19. Ibid., 18.

20. Ibid., 44.

21. Ibid., 74.

22. Derek Kidner, *Psalms 1–72* (Downers Grove: IVP, 1973), 237.

23. The material used here is taken from "Betty and John Stam Martyred," *Christianity.com*, http://www.christianity.com/ChurchHistory/11630759, accessed August 24, 2011.

24. Found online at http://www.carlstam.org/familyheritage/jbstam.html.

25. Daniel Bays, "Christianity in China," *Christian History Magazine*. Issue 98, http://www.christianhistorymagazine.org/wp-content/wS8wVsy62N/chm98-gBf0t.pdf, accessed August 24, 2011.

26. Taylor., 116.

27. Taylor, 122–23.

28. Ibid,, 123.

29. Ibid., 123–24.

30. Ibid., 108–9.

Chapter 10

1. Eileen Crossman, *Mountain Rain*, (Singapore: OMF, 1982), 4.

2. Mrs. Howard Taylor, *Behind the Ranges* (London: CIM, 1944), 44.

3. Crossman, 11.

4. Ibid., 67–68

5. Ibid., 89.

6. Taylor, 27.

7. Ibid., 32–33.

8. Ibid., 58.

9. James Fraser, *Prayer of Faith* (Littleton, CO: OMF, 2008), 11.

10. Ibid., 129

11. Fraser, 7.

12. John Piper, *A Hunger for God* (Wheaton: Crossway, 2007), 150.

13. Crossman, 111.

14. Ibid., 143.

15. Ibid., 145.

16. Ibid., 198.

17. Quoted from Re-Imagining Conference; Minneapolis, 1993.

18. This quote and the preceding quotes in this paragraph are taken from Al Mohler, "Is the Apostolic Preaching of the Cross Insane?" AlberMohler.com, entry posted April 6, 2007, http://www.albertmohler.com/2007/04/06/is-the-apostolic-preaching-of-the-cross-insane, accessed on October 7, 2010.

19. Crossman, 68.

20. Ibid., 20.

21. Ibid., 69.

22. Ibid., 104.

23. Ibid., 146.

24. Ibid.

25. Ibid., 147.

26. Ibid., 232.

27. Ibid., 72–73.

28. Ibid., 18–19.

29. Ibid., 106–7.

30. Ibid., 108.

31. Ibid., 234–35.

32. Taylor, 23.

33. Crossman, 204.

34. Ibid., 236

35. Ibid., 3.

36. Ibid., 237.

37. Fraser, 30.